Constitutional

Independent

A State Ratified Federal Limit Amendment, Need A 3rd Party? Constitutional Federal Government

By: B. J. Galt

Open Copyright

This publication may be reproduced or transmitted in any form or by any means, electronic or mechanical including photocopying, recording information storage, email or retrieval system.

PREFACE: Constitutional Independent

America represents a unique, shining example in government. Its success is the envy of people all over the world. The governmental concepts of freedom as defined in the US Constitution are powerful forces that generate unprecedented economic prosperity that is far greater than any other nation. For example: the national Gross Domestic Product (GDP) listed by the International Monetary Fund for some of the larger countries are:

United States	$15.5 Trillion
China	$5.8 Trillion
Japan	$5.4 Trillion
United Kingdom	$2.5 Trillion
Germany	$3.2 Trillion
France	$2.5 Trillion

American GDP is greater than China, Japan, the UK and Germany combined. Many countries depend on America for economic, charitable and military support. America is truly Atlas to the World! When faced with a $17+ Trillion unsustainable national debt, <u>Will Atlas be forced to shrug</u>?

PARTS

PART I

AMERICA IS ATLAS TO THE WORLD

America represents a unique, shining example in government. Its success is the envy of people all over the world. Its history is proof that "freedom to pursue happiness" is a powerful incentive. This simple, governmental concept defined in the US Constitution is a powerful force that generates unprecedented economic prosperity that is far greater than any other nation.

For example: the national Gross Domestic Product (GDP) listed by the International Monetary Fund for some of the larger countries are:

United States	$15.5 Trillion
China	$5.8 Trillion
Japan	$5.4 Trillion
Germany	$3.2 Trillion
France	$2.5 Trillion
United Kingdom	$2.2 Trillion

This country in a period of 230+ years has risen to such heights as to possess over 60 percent of the world's wealth while having only about 7 percent of the world's population? The economy of the United States is greater than the economies of Japan, Germany, China, the United Kingdom and France **combined.**

As a result of this unprecedented success, many countries depend on America for military, economic and charitable support.

Where in the world is our Military?   On 700+ bases in 135 nations according to an article in the American Legion Magazine.

Some of the largest are:
Republic of Korea 27,000
Japan   50,000
Iraq   15,000 (In Embassy 2012)
Kuwait   16,000
Hawaii   35,000
Afghanistan   100,000
United Kingdom 10,000
Germany   58,000
Italy   10,000
Alaska   19,000
Continental US 876,000
At sea/in port 115,000

Consider the industry, logistics, facilities and equipment costs to support the Military Complex. The proposed 2014 Federal Military Budget is $632 Billion. The United States spends more on its military than any other nation in the world. In 2009, the United States military budget accounted for almost 40% of the world's military spending. Its defense budget is nearly six times larger than that of China, even though China's army is almost double the size of the United States.

European NATO members continue to spend, on average, well under 2 % of gross domestic product (GDP) on defense, according to figures provided by the Atlantic Alliance. The average for European allies is 1.7 %, while the US GDP allotment in 2009 was 4%. The US spends more per capita than any other NATO member. In fact, the US last year spent about 44% more on defense than all other NATO members combined.

The U.S. has been the largest financial supporter of the U.N. since the organization's founding in 1945. The U.S. is currently assessed 22 percent of the U.N. regular budget and more than 27 percent of the U.N. peacekeeping budget. In dollar terms, the Administration's budget for FY 2011 requested $516.3 million for the U.N. regular budget and more than $2.182 billion for the peacekeeping budget.

America is truly Atlas to the World! Will it be possible for America to continue in this role without threatening its future?

The 2013 $3.8 Trillion Federal Budget with a projected $680 Billion deficit adding to the $16 equaling over a $17 Trillion Federal debtn clearly indicates a Federal Government that is fiscally out of control.

Future unfunded liabilities in Social Security and Medicare and the new Health Reform Bill will continually add to the Federal debt creating fiscal conditions that threaten insolvency and the survival of the United States of America. **Will Atlas America be forced to shrug?**

What is needed is **Recurrence to Fundamental Principles**" which is periodically essential to the maintenance of a free society. This book will present the example of a new Federalist check and balance; a State ratified "Federal Limit Amendment". Also >40 initiatives are proposed to reestablish truly constitutional operation of the Federal Government. The need for a 3rd party is *al*so considered.

PART II

THE PROBLEM: EXCESSIVE GOVERNMENT

America today is facing an internal danger that is far greater than any external threat posed by any hostile nation. It is a corrosive, deadly danger. If left unchecked, it will certainly cause the downfall of this great nation. It is difficult in this age of an "affluent society", where "instant gratification" is prevalent, to believe that such an eventual downfall could occur. But the lessons of human history have clearly proven that it surely will happen unless our course is changed. This is not some far off danger. It is quite possible that we who are living today may witness the end of the American dream of freedom for the individual and "government of the people, by the people and for the people".

CORRUPTIVE BIG GOVERNMENT

The 2013 $3.8 Trillion Federal Budget is simply too large to be effectively managed. Even worse, these massive funds and the related federal powers they represent corrupt federal representative politicians and bureaucrats. This was clearly demonstrated when the Republicans came to control the Presidency and the legislative branches with majorities. Access to all that money and power turned them into fiscally irresponsible spenders

President Bush added to the problem by never vetoing any Republican spending bill. He authorized the Iraq and Afghanistan wars, the Part D Medication program, the Economic Stimulus Act of 2008 and the TARP bank bailout, all without budgetary funding, thereby allowing unprecedented deficits to be created.

When the Republicans succumbed to these attractions, they lost their reputation as the party of constitutional small government and low taxes and thereby they lost the Conservative faithful. Republicans did not change government, government changed the party. The question for the Republicans now is, can they reestablish their previous reputation in a believable way? Their loss of the Presidential Campaign of 2012 gives them even less credibility.

In the first year of the Obama administration, the expansion of government was on steroids. Using the Democratic congressional majorities and Presidency the $800 Billion American Recovery and Reinvestment Act of 2009 was passed to stimulate the economy. Mostly it has used to stimulate and grow the Federal Government. It has failed to effectively improve the unemployment conditions. Its main effect has been to expand the number of Federal employees and bolster state budgets. So it is not surprising that this massive government directed spending had little effect in improving the recession and related private sector job prospects.

Bailout funding of General Motors and Chrysler extended Federal power into the private sector as never before seen.

The Obama administration and Democratic congressional majority also passed the 2500 page Affordable Care Act (Obama Care) with future implications of massive increases in Federal controls, bureaucracies and related costs.

The 2013 $3.8 Trillion Federal Budget with a projected $680 Billion deficit adding to the $16 Trillion Federal debt clearly indicates a Federal Government that is fiscally out of control.

Future unfunded liabilities in Social Security and Medicare and the new Health Reform Bill will continually add to the Federal debt creating fiscal conditions that threaten survival of the United States of America.

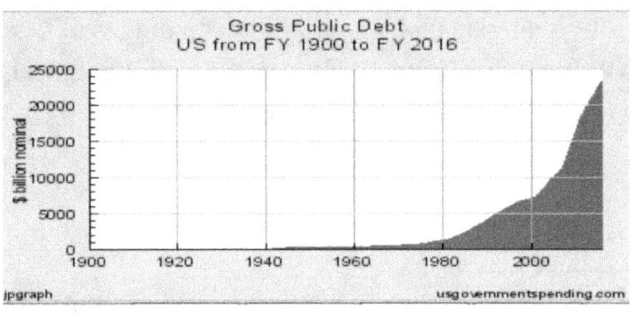

The 2013 Federal debt is $17+ Trillion. Continuing Deficit spending adds to the debt every year. Insolvency due to growing debt interest payments is a real possibility. Neither party proposes balanced budgets . Over the next 10 years, $8+ Trillion will be added to the debt.

What will we pass on to our grandchildren; unfillable program promises, massive, uncontrollable government and unsustainable national debts?

All of the budget plans proposed by the Democrats or Republicans only address reducing the budget deficit (the amount over a balanced budget). These plans only reduce the amount of budget growth. Small reductions are made over a 10 year period. No meaningful cuts are made now. These plans require that future legislators must do the actual cutting to reduce possible budget growth.

None of the plans actually reduce the $17 Trillion current national debt. In fact, even if the proposed cuts are actually done over the 10 year period, $7 – 8 Trillion more will be added to the debt because budgets will not be balanced during this period.

How long can this go on before funding realities will force insolvency? How will our children deal with these generational debt burdens?

GOVERNMENT TOO BIG TO SURVIVE?

We hear that some financial and auto companies are too big to be allowed to fail because, if they fail, there will be national and international catastrophic, systemic effects. It is actually possible that they are too big to survive. The same can be said of the Federal Government with its enormous size, management structures, inefficiencies and future debt potentials.

We have had the Tech Bubble, the Housing Bubble, now we have the Government Bubble. By their nature, bubbles are always temporary and then they burst. The Government Bubble is more like a balloon. But it too has expansion limits beyond which it will burst. Limit control is essential for survival.

The **Peter Principle** is the principle that "In a bureaucracy, everyone tends to rise to their level of incompetence". Formulated by Dr. Lawrence Peter in his 1968 book *"The Peter Principle"*. This principle has real validity. It holds that in a bureaucracy of government or business, members are promoted so long as they work competently. Sooner or later they are promoted to a position at which they are no longer competent (their "level of incompetence"), and there they remain.

Peter's corollary states that "in time, every post tends to be occupied by an employee who is incompetent to carry out his duties" and adds that "work is then accomplished by those employees who have not yet reached their level of incompetence".

This principle and problem is very true in government as well as private sector bureaucracies. In fact, the problem is made worse by the difficulty in eliminating unionized, incompetent government workers as well as the tendencies of government departments to perpetually expand. These departments will always ensure that their budgets are fully spent so they will not be reduced, and they will promote efforts to justify their expansion in the next budget cycle.

The evolution and expansion of Social Security, Medicare and Medicaid illustrate the truth of these principles. Not only have they been expanded to levels of mismanagement, the trust funds intended to effectively fund these programs have been raided, transferring their funds to general spending programs. So now these programs are in jeopardy of inadequate funding and in need of major reforms to keep them solvent. Both parties are reluctant to address these reform needs because of the political implications of having to reduce or significantly change the programs and then deal with the related reactions from the program beneficiaries.

The Affordable Care Act (Obama Care) further expands the role of the Federal Government to even higher levels of economic and health care involvement. The examples of its passage and start up illustrate how inept and incompetent massive bureaucracies can be.

To the size of a state there is a limit, as there is to plants, animals and implements, for they can none of them retain their facility when they are too large.

Aristotle

Loss of Governmental Control

The danger for America is that of the people losing control of their government and the directly related effect; the creation of excessive, inefficient, burdensome, character-crushing government. This danger is already extensive in its implementation and it is capable of exponentially increasing its growth rate in proportion to the degree of its prevalence. This is especially true about the Federal Government. State governments have also grown proportionally and have similar entrenched personnel problems. But they represent a lesser danger because they are more subject to local control and many have constitutional requirements to meet balanced budget requirements.

Effective governmental control requires concern and action on the part of the people and this is exactly what is lacking. Now, if you are like the majority of Americans, you are probably thinking, "Oh no, another lecture on the importance of being active in politics and informed on governmental functions". Your thinking will be indicative of the fact that the millions of such messages aimed at arousing you to political participation have been and really are quite ineffective. If you doubt the extent of the general unconcern for government and politics, then you probably have never tried to recruit party workers or stimulate citizen civic action. The apathy is massive as demonstrated by the minimal turn out in elections. The apathy is especially notable with the youth age 30 and under.

They see representatives who disregard their election promises once elected and are too influenced by lobbyists and political pressures. Most youths have no faith that Social Security benefits will be there when they need them. Projections indicate that they are well justified in these beliefs. The Social Security System has been receiving more than is paid out for many years. However these surpluses were not allowed to accumulate in a Trust Fund as authorized thereby creating a well financed system. Instead the Congress has used and continues to use the surpluses for general budget expenses and provides IOU's to the Social Security trust accounts for these funds. With the Federal budget running deficits and expanding debt, these IOU's are meaningless in value.

Being realistic about it, most Americans openly state that they do not like to discuss politics or government. Nor do they do party work or write to editors or to their Congressmen. In other words, they have ceased trying to be influential in the control of their government. These citizens feel that if they pay a reasonable amount of attention to the issues as expressed through the various news media around election time and if they go to vote (many will not even do that), they are doing all that they must. In any case, again realistically, these things are all that they will do. And yet, paradoxically, the American people, on the whole, are undoubtedly the best informed, best educated and most industrious of all the people of the world.

How can this be? How can this great people, possessed of such literacy and the best communications that technology can provide be in danger of losing control of their government? The answer is simply that the government has become too large to be effectively controlled through elected representatives. Today, constitutionally defined checks and balances have been bypassed or made ineffective. President Obama uses Executive Orders to override or modify existing laws. The main error is in the abandonment of the constitutionally defined roles of State and Federal Government. The Federal Government, by virtue of its remote and extensive nature, presents by far the greatest present problem of control for the people. Its size exceeds the ability of the people to effectively comprehend its complexity and intelligently, democratically control it.

REPRESENTATIVE CONTROL

We expect to control our government at the federal level through our representatives, but this assumes that our representatives, in turn, truly can have control when elected. These lines of control seem extremely fragile when we consider that each of us can only vote for one senator and a congressional representative with each election. There are totals of 100 senators and 537 representatives who must control close to 3,000,000 federal employees and manage a $17 Trillion budget. The mind boggles at such expectations, especially if one recognizes that <u>most of these representatives' time is spent in the proposing and processing of new legislation and in raising money and working to be re-elected.</u>

Your money is spent through massive Appropriations Bills developed and promoted by lobbyists, passed by the Congress and signed by the President. The Government does not have any money. Through taxes, it takes money from you and borrows and prints more, then spends that! The Iraq and Afghanistan wars, the Part D Prescription Drug programs and The bailouts of 2008 and 2009 were all done with deficit spending. The Federal Debt in 2013 is $17+ Trillion. This is a debt that will burden future generations and can never be eliminated with taxation. As the Federal Reserve monetizes the debt by printing money, the dollar is devalued ultimately leading to hyper-inflation.

Expect to see continuing deficits in the foreseeable future, leading to much more debt. **Interest payments on that debt will become the largest item in the federal budget**. These alarming debt figures do not take into account the impact of the baby boomer spike in retiree populations that will lead to even more future enormous demands on

Social Security, Medicare and Medicaid funding requirements. With complete disregard for these debt considerations, additional major spending programs such as The Affordable Care Act and Climate (Energy) Change are promoted and passed.

Congressional oversight of government operations is not a major priority. Oversight is usually driven by political expediency or only in the case of gross discrepancies or corruption. If oversight does uncover ineffective operations that should be terminated, Congress is reluctant to do so due to the pressures from those receiving services from such operations and their lobbyists.

It would be accurate to say that this form of government is, in truth, more bureaucratic than representative. The fact that Congress is no longer reflecting public opinion was illustrated by the way the 2500+ page Affordable Care Act (Obama Care) was passed with little transparency, vote bribery and only Democrat party support.

Most people do not have a real sense of how much money and massive power a $17+ Trillion Federal Budget represents. Their minds cannot truly comprehend such large numbers. Along with the lobbyists, the special interests and entrenched bureaucracy involved, all this power and money has the potential to overwhelm and corrupt the best intentioned politicians.

Americans, who enjoy great material abundance and technical advancement, are well informed and generally well educated. They should be capable of effectively controlling their government and yet they are not. Their reluctance to enter into and become involved in politics and governmental matters stems directly from the overwhelming complexity, frustration and enormity of this problem of government size and control. The ineffectiveness of control through representation is clearly apparent and yet, few people really recognize this fact and fear its implications. The frustrations that they feel concerning the results they obtain through their representatives are reflected in their attitudes and comments concerning politics and politicians in general. They rightly feel that too often what politicians promise and what they deliver are two greatly different things.

Before election they hear glowing promises of new services, tax reductions and increases in government efficiencies so that truly needed functions can be established. But once in office, the actual desired accomplishments are minimal. Tax shuffling may be done, but in the end, the taxes are usually raised. New programs are initiated but a negligible number of inefficient, unnecessary, old programs are removed. So the net result is merely another increase in overall governmental functions.

These frustrations have caused the formation of the Tea Party Movement which finds membership from both political parties as well as independents and libertarians. Their expressed goal is for smaller, more responsive, Constitutional government. They are the "Taxed Enough Already" paarty.

GOVERNMENT - A DANGEROUS FORCE

The groove in this old recording of government unfaithfulness and ineffectiveness is worn deep and the bad fidelity of the sound is beginning to grate on the ears of the people. They are beginning to sense the truth of what George Washington said many years ago:

"Government is not reason, it is not eloquence. It is a force. Like fire, it is a dangerous servant and a fearful master".

The government, unless it can be made effectively responsive to the desires of the people, will continue to be an ever-growing force that will ultimately attain burdensome mastery over a dependent people and thereby cause the corruption and erosion of their character and strength. It is these latter effects on character that will ultimately cause the downfall of the nation.

This pattern of national degradation is not new to mankind. There is an abundance of historical and present examples. Examine the nations of the world, especially those in the European area that have intensively developed systems of socialistic government but still claim to be part of the free world. The individuals in such nations are frustrated and submerged under the smothering influences of governmental controls and heavy tax burdens. These nations have passed their peaks and are definitely in states of decline.

Socialism refers to a broad array of doctrines or political movements that envisage a socio-economic system in which property and the distribution of wealth are subject to government control. This control may be either directly exercised through popular collectives or indirectly exercised on behalf of the people by the state. As an economic system, socialism is often characterized by state or community ownership of the means of production.

GOVERNMENT IN ENGLAND

British MP Daniel Hannan in his book "The Plan" describes the effects of excessive Socialist government in the United Kingdom:

"The British state is failing. It cannot deliver even the most basic services competently. We have the highest prisoner population in Europe, and one of the highest crime rates. Our school children compare dismally with similarly aged pupils in other countries and in previous generations. Our healthcare system is more likely to kill its charges than any other in the developed world. Our roads are choked, our railways crumbling, our airports unbearable. Our borders are, to all intents and purposes, wide open."

"The state has become so large and unwieldy, the number of officials benefiting from the status quo so great, that no single minister, be he the most energetic in Whitehall, can refashion it. So what is going wrong? Why does the state fail? The answer is that modern government is already running at capacity. It has taken too much on. It is literally unable to assume new functions and discharge them efficiently."

"As Kenneth Boulding put it: 'The larger and more authoritarian the organization, the better the chance that its top decision-makers will be operating in purely imaginary worlds'.

Friedrich   Hayek,   in   his   1944   economic treatise,"The Road to Serfdom", Hayek could see that centralization was unsuited to the complexities of modern administration.

MP Hannan's Plan proposed a 12-month legislative programme that is based on these three principles:

Decisions should be taken as closely as possible to the people who are affected by them.

Decision-makers should be directly accountable.

The citizen should be as free as possible from state coercion.

England, which was once a powerful empire and still claims to be one of the important leaders of the free world, exhibits a dangerously high level of socialistic governmental influence in its society. At the time of the national elections in 1966, it was estimated that one out of every four dwellings was owned by the government and that about 23 percent of the heads of households worked for the government. Remarkable as this is, the liberal Labor Party won an overwhelming victory, thereby increasing their margin of seats in the Parliament from three to one hundred. Prime Minister Wilson, at that time, claimed this to be a mandate which he would use to put through his party's programs. Needless to say, these programs have further extended governmental influences within their society.

At the 2010 election, the Conservative Party won an absolute majority of MPs representing English constituencies, with 298 out of 533.

Monetary devaluation and price inflation pose constant threats for the British economy. Corrective measures, which include higher taxes and governmental wage and price controls, are commonly advocated but little is suggested or accomplished to reduce governmental spending or its influence in the economy. In fact, if the tax advocates have their way, more money will be provided for more government spending, etc., etc. The average Britton must in fact be frugal by American standards in order to live on what is left after taxes. Yet he is told to be even more Spartan to stem inflation; while the real culprit, government spending, goes unchecked.

The effects of this over-government in Great Britain present a classic, present-day example of the related deteriorating effects. Ferdinand Fauber, the Toledo Blade foreign correspondent in London, in an article entitled, "Why Is 'Saving Pound' Routine?", lists the following attitudes as being prevalent in the general English business environment:

"The hard sell is vulgar. So is the rat race. Saturday work interferes with relaxation. The night shift idea is repulsive. A day's work should not lead to undue fatigue. It can be interrupted frequently for personal business. Stores close at the same time as offices, if not earlier. Hard work diminishes the stature of the individual."

From the want of a constitution in England to restrain and regulate the wild impulse of power, many of the laws are irrational and tyrannical and the administration of them vague and problematical.

Prime Minister Margaret Thatcher, the most conservative of Britain's leaders said, "The problem with Socialism is that you run out of other people's money."

We in America would be wise to study Britain's example and to relate it to developments in our country.

THE ROMAN EMPIRE

The best known example of national weakening and collapse is the Roman Empire. This once great society began initially as a highly decentralized government made up of provinces with each province having imperium unto itself. Augustus, in 27 BC, obtained sole imperium in a number of provinces and Constantine, from 284 to 337 AD, established sole imperium and absolute monarchy throughout the empire in all provinces. From that time on, there was no distinction of provinces.

The old Republic Aerarium (Congressional equivalent) became merely a municipal treasury. The officers of the Emperor's body guard became the great officers of the state. His private council became the supreme court of appeal. All power resided in him and he was looked to for all provisions. This centralized power caused a paralysis of effective administration, with a related corruption of officials at all levels. Municipal liberty was lost and with this came evil, repressive fiscal systems that caused the decay of the middle classes. Once this core strength was destroyed, complete disorganization set in, which facilitated the dismemberment of the empire and its eventual collapse.

THE GREEK EMPIRE

The same general pattern can be seen in the history of the Greek Empire. Its eventual collapse too can be traced to a decay of public spirit which led to corruption in public life and government. Especially noteworthy in the degradation of the Greek Empire was a loss of patriotism on the part of the people. As decay set into their society, they came to rely more and more on mercenaries for defense. They shirked their responsibilities in providing for the defense of their country. More importantly, they refused to bear their responsibilities concerning action in the control of their government.

Edith Hamilton wrote this about the decline of Athens; *"When the freedom they wished for most was freedom from responsibility, then Athens ceased to be free and was never free again."*

The biographer Plutarch, writing 500 years after the glories of classical Greece, lamented that in his time weeds grew amid the empty colonnades of the once-impressive Greek city-states.

Today, Greece is considered to be near bankruptcy requiring repeated bail outs to support operations having allowed its government to far exceed the capacity of its people to support it.

OTHER EXAMPLES

A "Life Line" article had this to say about patterns of national decay: *"The pages of history tell the story of twenty nations which have been free. Their average length of life has been just two centuries, two hundred years. The cycle has been plain to see. It has gone from slavery to spiritual faith; from spiritual faith to courage; from courage to liberty; from liberty to abundance; from abundance to complacency; from complacency to apathy; from apathy to dependency; and, tragically, from dependency back to slavery."*

Note: America is over 230 years old.

If we examine the history of America and current characteristics of attitude and reaction, it would seem we are entering into the Apathy stage. This is indicated by an increasing tendency on the part of the people to dependency and to withdraw from governmental concerns and assume an attitude that says; "What I do politically doesn't really mean anything anyway." Their reaction is a natural one when faced with a complex, entrenched and expansive bureaucracy governed by unresponsive representatives.

This pattern of degradation may be inevitable. Perhaps it is the nature of people to destroy their societies in this way. History says the odds are against us. But, if this is true, the American society will have an uneasy conscience as it passes through the last stages of Apathy and Dependence. This nation is the first nation in history that was formed with the dangers of excessive government clearly in mind. We are warned by our Constitution, The Bill of Rights and our founding history.

If our founding principles cannot be made to work, if our people cannot make sound readjustments and maintain effective control of their government, then there is no governmental system known to mankind that will not eventually be destroyed by its parental society.

EFFECTS OF OVER-GOVERNMENT

The expansion and centralization of governmental control is a dominant characteristic in countless examples of national history. Most of the older nations of the world reflect the effects of intensification and expansion of their governmental systems. Generally it can be said that those nations with the greatest centralization of government have the least freedom for the individual and furthermore exhibit the worst results in terms of what is desirable in society.

Some governments, such as the Communist type, can excel in certain areas of endeavor by using dictatorial force to generate powerful action. But as far as overall results go, they are complete failures. An especially noteworthy lack in such societies is that of intellectual and creative accomplishments. This lack develops because the pervasive governmental influences existent in such societies smother the will and drive of individuals. Since the total results of any society are directly related to the contributions of its individuals, the summed results and accomplishments of these societies fall far below their real potentials.

The History of the Soviet Union, the USSR begins with the Russian Revolution of 1917. Communism was implemented across the territories of the former Russian Empire. World War II devastated much of the USSR. One out of every three World War II deaths was a citizen of the Soviet Union. After World War II, the Soviet Union's armies occupied Eastern Europe, where Communist governments came to power in a Soviet bloc. After many years of the "Cold War", the Soviet Union collapsed in 1991 when Boris Yeltsin seized power. While losing control over many of its satellite nations, Russia has since struggled to establish a free market style economy within a democracy. The government still retains strong socialistic tendencies and even shows tendencies to reestablish controls over its satellite nations and a more autocratic government under Putin.

ECONOMIC SYMPTOMS OF EXCESSIVE GOVERNMENT

Another symptom of national sickness due to the smothering influences of government is in the area of economic ills. Where centralized government has the greatest influence in the business enterprises of its people, the economic ills will be the greatest. The government, through the development and application of excessive taxation and regulations, destroys the return to effort for the individual. It thereby proportionately reduces the willingness to give that bit of extra innovation and effort that makes the difference between a vibrant, successful society and one that is sluggish and weak.

The government, when it takes over the operation of businesses, short circuits the energy and stimulation and disciplines of free enterprise and free will. The result is a loss of extra individual efforts with the summed results suffering. Adam Smith, an economist of nearly two centuries ago, explained in his book, "The Wealth of Nations":

"It is only for the sake of profit that any man employs a capital in the support of industry; and he will always, therefore, endeavor to employ it in the support of that industry of which the produce is likely to be of the greatest value. He generally, indeed, neither intends it promote the public interest, nor knows how much he is promoting it. By directing that industry in such a manner as its produce may be of greatest value, he intends only his own gain, and he is in this, as in many other cases, led by an invisible hand to promote an end which has no part of his intention. Nor is it always the worse for society that it has no part in it."

Adam Smith's "invisible hand" functions intuitively through all the individuals and businesses dealing in the free market. This is why it represents the only working process that is capable of perpetually adjusting and improving mankind's economic situation for the good. Governments can never hope to achieve these perfections of control. They can and do upset and restrict these functions by excessive regulations and interferences.

The government will always become a poor manager of business functions because it does not have to respond to the discipline of competition. It also does not have to make a profit. If more money is required to meet operating expenses, more tax money or deficit funds are made available. It is in the fact that government becomes a bad manager that the danger exists.

When the government begins any new service or operation, it does so usually for only the soundest of reasons. These reasons must be relatively sound or the necessary legislation to establish the new function would never be passed. The supporting Legislators involved are, for the most part, honest and intelligent leaders who are responding to a demand. So in the beginning, these new functions are usually worthwhile and productive because they are specifically designed to fit the immediate need. But lacking the discipline of free competition and the necessity to make a profit, the incentives to manage wisely and efficiently are not present. So, unwarranted expansion, inefficiency and waste set in. The operation is usually never effectively corrected unless the problems reach scandalous proportions.

Also, the bureaucrats who manage such new functions, along with the beneficiaries, became lobbyists and pressuring influences that cause these operations to expand gradually to proportions far beyond the original intent. Efforts are made to be sure to spend any budgetary funds provided. If they don't, their next budget allocation will be reduced. So rather than effectively managing expenditures, requests for similar or usually expanding budget requests are typical. What is lacking is an effective means of limiting needless expansion of such functions and a means of accomplishing effective oversight and periodic review and rejustification to ensure effective operations and a continuing real need.

SOCIAL EFFECTS OF EXCESSIVE GOVERNMENT

For excessive governmental intensification to take place, it is essential that the people become gradually willing to give up their rights and freedoms and to compromise their principles. A drift toward rule flexibility and away from guiding ideals is part of the pattern of national degradation. It is clearly evident in the histories of fallen nations and, to a large extent, in our own modern, national trends. The cultural and religious life in our society is especially symptomatic of weakening moral strength. Fundamental religious principles that have given mankind strength through the centuries are diluted with materialistic sophistication till they become meaningless. The beauty and art of the ages is rejected in favor of transient modern experimentation and radical expression. The enduring positive inheritances from the past speak of strength and depth and those who are weak in character and moral courage are made uncomfortable by their examples.

INTERNATIONAL EFFECTS OF EXCESSIVE GOVERNMENT

Usually the intensification of government within a society corresponds directly to a loss of national internal strength and international stature. This pattern is clearly evident in many of the European nations. It can also be said that the United States has sustained definite losses in stature and dignity. These losses have especially been notable during the recent years when the greatest expansions and centralization of government power have taken place. Our foreign embassies and offices have been abused and damaged and embassy personnel killed. Our word and promises of support have been found to be undependable. We have been forced to withdraw from strategic locations and have allowed the establishment of enemy strongholds in this hemisphere and near our shores.

We have been judged as being economically irresponsible, as is evidenced by general concern over the size of the national debt and the deteriorating value of the dollar. Rating agencies down grade our debt ratings. Those who would fund our debts are concerned about these trends and are more and more reluctant to continue lending to meet our needs. We look back on these trends, actions and events and rationalize how they could have happened, but the pattern is clear. The Federal

Government has grown beyond reasonable constitutional limits. Our weak responses indicate a deteriorating national fiber or, more basically, a general loss of character on the part of the people.

FREEDOM - THE INDIVIDUAL AND GOVERNMENT

About the time our original 13 states adopted their new Constitution, in 1787, Alexander Tyler, a Scottish history professor at the University of Edinburgh, had this to say about the fall of the Athenian Republic some 2,000 years prior:

"A democracy is always temporary in nature; it simply cannot exist as a permanent form of government."

"A democracy will continue to exist up until the time that voters discover that they can vote themselves generous gifts from the public treasury. From that moment on, the majority always votes for the candidates who promise the most benefits from the public treasury, with the result that every democracy will finally collapse due to loose fiscal policy, which is followed by a dictatorship."

"The average age of the worlds greatest ivilizations from the beginning of history, has been about 200

years. During those 200 years, these nations always progressed through the following sequence:

1. From bondage to spiritual faith;

2. From spiritual faith to great courage;
3. From courage to liberty;
4. From liberty to abundance;
5. From abundance to complacency;
6. From complacency to apathy;
7. From apathy to dependence;
8. From dependence back into bondage "

The United States is now somewhere between the "complacency and apathy" phase of democracy, with some 45+ percent of the nation's population already having reached the "governmental dependency" phase.

The critical point is when the number of people receiving on government entitlements passes 50% and can control future elections. Today, 45% of US citizens pay no income tax. From that point, the party that promises the most free entitlements wins.

Unfortunately, less than 50% of the population will soon be paying the taxes to support the majority. It will not be long after that the country will be bankrupt. If one considers the current $17+ Trillion National Debt and continuing $1 Trillion+

annual deficits along with all the unfunded liabilities, actual insolvency could be in the near future.

Then, Atlas America will have to shrug its world support and reduce its national services.

One can look at history and see how these patterns of national rise and decline would indicate that citizens living in a democracy will always governmentalize their society to extinction. A feeling of inevitability can be developed. But our forefathers wrote the Constitution so that, supposedly, we would be able to exercise effective restraints and controls. This section will examine some of these principles and guides.

FREEDOM AND INCENTIVES

Government destroys incentive and character through the excessive application of taxation, controls and welfare dependency. Note that it is excessive applications that are destructive. Certain appropriate taxation, control and safty net functions are undeniably necessary in any orderly society. But it is in politicians tendency to succumb to the power to excessively expand these functions that the danger exists.

Of these three, excessive welfare/dependency functions are the most destructive of human character. Welfare functions require the most personal and close supervision and administration. If welfare dispensations are allowed to go to the undeserving indiscriminately, people will be attracted to such easy sustenance and, once they are partakers, they will gradually lose personal drive and ambition. The close, personal aspect of these functions makes it imperative that they be performed as a local, or no higher than a state function.

Excessive taxation destroys incentive and mainly attacks the producers in society. It is the producer's hope of personal gain that drives them. If the fruits of their labor are severely limited, they will have a proportionately diminished ambition. Incentives can also be smothered by excessive government controls, regulations and influences. Complaints about this sort of excess are common in today's business environment, especially among the small, individually owned businesses.

Regulations work like taxes. It makes no difference to the entrepreneur, or the economy, whether the entrepreneur must write a $5,000 check to the government for taxes or a $5,000 check to comply with a regulation. Forcing the entrepreneur to comply with unnecessary regulations diverts resources to less-productive uses.

The key element in any society is each individual. To the extent that freedom to choose and perform constructive works is retained and to the extent that citizens benefit from the results of their works, to that extent will the summed constructive benefits for society grow. For, if each individual can freely choose work and have the greatest incentive for doing it, they will make the greatest effort that their particular nature and talents will allow.

Eric Hoffer, in his book "The Ordeal of Change", drew on his studies of past societies to comment on bureaucratic influences on free trade:

"*In a scribe dominated society the trader is regulated off the face of the earth. When the scribe comes into power he derives a rare satisfaction from tearing tangible things out of the hands of practical people and harnessing these people to the task of achieving the impossible and often killing them in the process.*"

A WELFARE ENVIRONMENT

If an environment develops where welfare becomes a way of life, such as we see in the slums and urban core areas of larger cities, the people in these areas will become semi-permanent wards of the government. They and their children especially, will learn and come to believe that sustenance can be had for nothing.

We should not be surprised at the unrest in the slum areas of our cities. The youth in these areas have learned and now expect a reasonably comfortable life without working for it. Many have seen their elders live this way and have been promised better conditions under more welfare by our governmental leaders.

Those adults in poverty areas who suffer from physical disabilities or who live under handicaps of racial or ethnic discrimination deserve help. Few will disagree that valid needs exist. So, the great and important question is how to create selective, effective aid programs for those who need and deserve help. The keys to success in such programs lie in the personal touch and in the extent of aids given. Welfare actions must be locally designed and carefully administered so as to be truly effective and to minimize their destructive effects.

Massive, poorly administered doles with minimal qualification will only create masses of kept citizens who will little resemble free and independent human beings. Politicians who advocate massive federal programs to solve slum problems do not recommend sound solutions, but are seeking to create gigantic power structures in which to shelter their kept constituency.

Indiscriminate welfare functions that give sustenance to the undeserving poor will not make them deserving, but will encourage them in their sloth and intemperance. What is even worse, by funding such ill-place welfare through taxation of the productive people in society, only evil effects are created at all levels of the society. The undeserving will be rewarded and the productive are discouraged from greater efforts.

LAW AND FREEDOM

The individual must be restrained from committing irresponsible, criminal acts that are harmful to other members of the society. Laws and government functions that are created to provide this sort of control generally improve a society's basic character. If the law solely functions to provide protection for individual rights, it will not go wrong. It is only when government takes up the role of resolver of social and economic inequalities that it enters dangerous waters. For then the people must form pressure groups to insist that they receive their shares. Others seeing this will react with further organized demonstrations and demands and still others will do likewise, ad infinitum. More and more functions must be established to satisfy these groups.

The police and militia, instead of putting their full effort toward fighting crime and keeping peace, will become more and more involved in quelling riots and controlling demonstrations. Thus, law enforcement and social order collapses. The pattern is as old as Rome and Athens and still we make the same mistakes.

The concept of freedoms and incentives for the individual as being the ideal catalysts to generate a vibrant, successful society is not unique to America. Remember that the free world's governments also have freedom for the individual defined as a basic element of their constitutions and yet none have matched our success.

Why then has this country in a period of 230 years risen to such heights as to possess over 60 percent of the world's wealth while having only about 7 percent of the world's population?

The economy of the United States is greater than the economies of Japan, Germany, China, the United Kingdom and France combined.

Why is the US so exceptional and successful? We hear many reasons and theories as to why this is true. Freedom for the individual is undoubtedly a very important one, but there is another about which we hear less and less as the years go by. This reason is probably more important than freedom for the individual, for its purpose is to retain freedom and incentives for the individual. This reason is governmental restraint. It was written into our Constitution and Bill of Rights and, up to about sixty years ago, it was very effective.

CONSTITUTIONAL RESTRAINTS

The Constitution of the United States is unique among the constitutions of the world in the way it was written to restrict the Federal Government from interfering with the rights of individuals. Contrast the way the Russian Constitution is written with the way the American Constitution is written.

Article 125 of the Russian Constitution states:

"In Conformity with the interests of the working people and in order to strengthen the Socialist system, the citizens of the USSR are guaranteed by law: (a) Freedom of speech; (b) Freedom of the press; (c) Freedom of assembly, including the holding of mass meetings; (d) Freedom of street processions and demonstrations."

These civil rights are ensured by placing at the disposal of the working people and their organizations; printing presses, communications facilities, and other material requisites for the exercise of these rights.

In contrast, the United States Constitution states:

"Congress shall make no Law...abridging the freedom of speech, or of the press; or the right of the people peaceably to assemble, and to petition the government for redress of grievances," and "the right of the people to be secure in their persons, houses, papers and effects shall not be violated and no person shall be deprived of life, liberty or property without due process of law; nor shall private property be taken for public use without just compensation".

Section 8 of the US Constitution defines the authorized powers of the Federal Government:

The Congress shall have power to lay and collect taxes, duties, imposts and excises, to pay the debts and provide for the common defense and general welfare of the United States; but all duties, imposts and excises shall be uniform throughout the United States;

To borrow money on the credit of the United States;

To regulate commerce with foreign nations, and among the several states, and with the Indian tribes;

To establish a uniform rule of naturalization, and uniform laws on the subject of bankruptcies throughout the United States;

To coin money, regulate the value thereof, and of foreign coin, and fix the standard of weights and measures;

To provide for the punishment of counterfeiting the securities and current coin of the United States;

To establish post offices and post roads;

To promote the progress of science and useful arts, by securing for limited times to authors and inventors the exclusive right to their respective writings and discoveries;

To constitute tribunals inferior to the Supreme Court;

To define and punish piracies and felonies committed on the high seas, and offenses against the law of nations;

To declare war, grant letters of marque and reprisal, and make rules concerning captures on land and water;

To raise and support armies, but no appropriation of money to that use shall be for a longer term than two years;

To provide and maintain a navy;

To make rules for the government and regulation of the land and naval forces;

To provide for calling forth the militia to execute the laws of the union, suppress insurrections and repel invasions;

To provide for organizing, arming, and disciplining, the militia, and for governing such part of them as may be employed in the service of the United States, reserving to the states respectively, the appointment of the officers, and the authority of training the militia according to the discipline prescribed by Congress;

To exercise exclusive legislation in all cases whatsoever, over such District (not exceeding ten miles square) as may, by cession of particular states, and the acceptance of Congress, become the seat of the government of the United States, and to exercise like authority over all places purchased by the consent of the legislature of the state in which the same shall be, for the erection of forts, magazines, arsenals, dockyards, and other needful buildings;--And

To make all laws which shall be necessary and proper for carrying into execution the foregoing powers, and all other powers vested by this Constitution in the government of the United States, or in any department or officer thereof.

Amendments IX and X were added in the BILL of Rights to further clarify the restrictive nature of the Constitution. Amendment IX states:

"The enumeration in the Constitution of certain rights shall not be construed to deny or disparage others retained by the people."

Amendment X states:

"The powers not delegated to the United States by the Constitution, nor prohibited by it to the States, are reserved to the States respectively, or to the people."

The difference would seem to be abundantly clear. Under the Communist/Socialist forms of government, the national government provides the rights for the people. Under the American Constitutional form of government, the Federal Government is restricted from interfering with these rights.

The Constitution of the United States more severely limits the powers and extent of the government than any ever has before. It is this restraint of government, combined with resulting freedom and incentives for the individual that have caused this country to achieve the success it has.

The checks and balances of government defined by the Constitution and the severe limitations placed on the Federal Government are fundamental keys in this matter of control. Our present danger lies in the fact that these restraints and restrictions have been weakened and voided and are being made meaningless.

CHECKS AND BALANCES

Most Americans recognize the fact that the roles of State and Federal Government no longer reflect a balance of power such as is defined in the Constitution. The Federal Government is steadily assuming more and more of the state duties and powers as time passes. Through liberal interpretations of the "General Welfare" and Commerce clauses in the Constitution, the Federal Government has moved in to deal with problems concerning education, public utilities, banking, insurance, business, agriculture, social welfare and a multitude of other areas that find no clear authorization in the Constitution.

Most would agree that these functions would be best performed at state or local levels. This is not possible as conditions presently exist. The states have reached their limits of taxing power and cannot properly respond to the problems that arise.

The only governmental power that can step forward to provide answers is the Federal Government. Through taxation, deficit budgeting policies, monetary printing and devaluation, bonding and borrowing policies, and other fiscal tactics money is obtained to provide the ability to respond. Thus the Federal Government establishes an ever-increasing role in these activities in spite of the fact that all reason says that they are best and most efficiently dealt with at state and local levels,

As the functions of the Federal Government became ever more encompassing and expansive, the ability and desire of the people to effectively control them decreases. This is true because it is natural for government to expand itself and with such expansion comes a complexity and diffusion that the representatives and people cannot effectively cope with. Thus, paradoxically, as the complexity increases, frustration causes the people to relinquish their responsibilities and retreat from governmental and political concerns. The danger in these diametrically opposed and equally destructive actions on the part of the government and people was clearly recognized by the founders of our country. It is for this reason that the founders established checks and balances and roles for State and Federal Governments as they did in the Constitution.

Unfortunately, it is clear that the checks and balances are not functioning as intended by the Constitutional authors. The Federal Government is now a massive complex with incomprehensible powers. The expansive forces within this structure in combination with the beneficiaries of its programs and influences represent explosive potentials for government growth.

Ronald Reagan said, the most frightening words a citizen can hear is *"I'm from the Federal Government and I'm here to help you."*

He also said *"It is not that we are taxed to little, it is that the government spends too much"*.

The cry of a dying society is *"Stop saving me!"*

GROWTH OF THE FEDERAL GOVERNMENT

Growth of Federal Spending and Employment

In 1910 the Federal Budget was 2.6% of total personal income.

There were 349,600 Federal employees.

By 1960 the Federal Budget was 21% of total personal income.

There were 2,580,000 Federal employees.

By 2003 the Federal Budget was 23% of total personal income.

There were 3,000,000 Federal employees.

In 2006 the Bureau of Economic Analysis reported that the average annual wage for civilian Federal employees was $106,579. This is twice the average annual compensation paid in the private sector of $53,289.

Since 1990, average compensation for Federal workers has increased by 129% as compared to 74% for private sector workers.

Leonard E. Read defined another way that government finances its operations besides taxation, **Inflation**:

"Whenever the take of the people's earned income by government reaches a certain level—20 or 25 percent—it is no longer politically expedient to pay for the costs of government by direct tax levies. Governments then resort to inflation as a means of financing their ventures. By "inflation" I mean increasing the volume of money by the national government's fiscal policy.

Governments resort to inflation with popular support because the people apparently are naive enough to believe that they can have their cake and eat it, too. Many people do not realize that they cannot continue to enjoy so-called "benefits" from government without having to pay for them. They do not appreciate the fact that inflation is probably the most unjust and cruelest tax of all.

What precisely is this disease that causes inflation and all these other troubles? It has many popular names, such as socialism, communism, state interventionism, and welfare statism. It has some local names: New Deal, Fair Deal, New Republicanism, New Frontier, Progressivism and the like."

The U.S. started to gradually move away from the Gold Standard with the adoption of the Bretton Woods system after World War II. With the Bretton Woods Agreement, the world's currencies were pegged to the dollar, which in turn was pegged to Gold at a rate of $35 per ounce.

Under President Nixon the Bretton Woods establishment began to crumble. Pressure took hold on the U.S. to abandon Bretton Woods, so international currencies could be freely valued on the market. The U.S. unilaterally terminated Bretton Woods in 1971, causing the U.S. dollar to effectively become the "reserve currency" for every country Today, most currencies in the world freely float against one another (many are still pegged to the U.S. dollar such as the Chinese Yuan), with sentiment rising or falling based on current account deficits, economic conditions, interest rates, and more.

New dollars are issued when the Federal Reserve elects to fund the purchase of debt, primarily U.S. Treasury Bonds, by creating new reserves rather than financing the purchase with existing reserves.

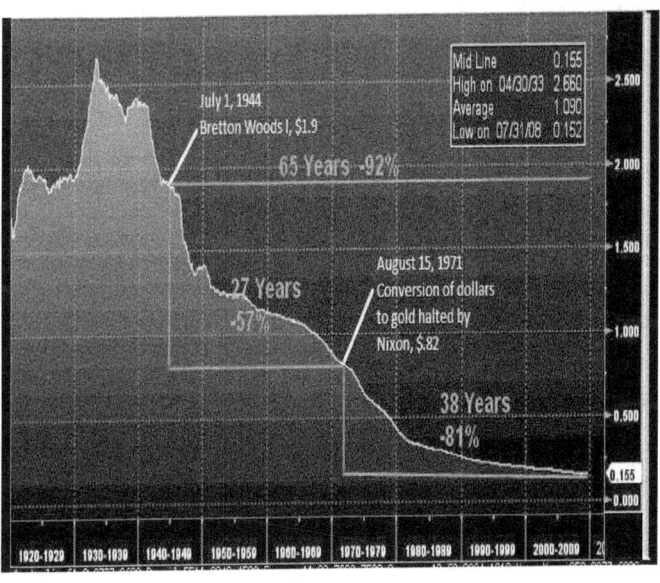

Dollar Purchasing Power Devaluation

Notice, this chart only goes to the year 2000. How much more has the purchasing power of the dollar been devalued in the last 12 years with the Federal Reserve printing money to stimulate the economy? Today the value of an ounce of gold is $1,200 +.

The Heritage Foundation provides an excellent source for statistics about the Federal Government revenue and spending from Federal Census and Budget reports.

Following are some summary statistical facts from those studies that give a sense of Federal Government growth.

In 1900, the US population was 76 million. The Federal Budget was $525 million or $6.90 per person. By 1940, the US population was132 million. The Federal Budget was then $5 Billion or $105 per person. By 1970, the US population was 210 million. The Federal Budget was then $200 Billion or $956 per person.

Federal Revenue, by Major Source, 1960-2006

Federal tax revenue has more than tripled since 1962. But federal spending has quadrupled.

Since 1962, federal tax revenue and spending have soared, increasing by over $1.5 Trillion and almost $2 Trillion, respectively. The government spent more than it took in during the vast majority of this period, generating an average annual deficit of $222 Billion since 1962. (The 2009 Federal Budget was $3.6 Trillion.)

Despite tax cuts, the federal tax burden per household is over 60% higher today than in 1960. American taxpayers are sending more of their household income to Washington even with President Bush's tax cuts, which took effect in 2001 and 2003. For 2005, the average household will pay $19,006, down from $21,939 in 2000 but much higher than $11,558 in 1960.

The average American household tax burden has increased steadily since 1962, rising 20 percent during the Clinton Administration. Today's tax burden remains higher than all Administrations except for Clinton, even with the recent tax cuts.

Federal spending per household soared by more than $8,000 between the Administrations of President John F. Kennedy and President George W. Bush.

The most dramatic decline in the top individual income tax rate occurred during the Reagan Administration - falling from 70 percent to 28 percent. It is now 35%.

Percentage Growth of Federal Spending and Inflation (Consumer Price Index), 1992-2005.

Total nominal spending has increased over 2,000 percent while the Consumer Price Index has increased only a little over 500 percent since 1962. Less than half of the increase in federal spending came from defense and homeland security spending.

The past four years have seen the sharpest growth in spending per household since the Johnson Administration, when the Great Society programs were enacted.

Federal spending has increased 290 percent since 1962, five times faster than median income, which has risen 54 percent.

Total Discretionary Spending vs. Mandatory Spending, 1962-2006.

Discretionary spending -- the portion of the budget subject to annual review and appropriation -- has risen 116 percent since 1962. Mandatory spending, consisting mostly of entitlements not subject to annual review and appropriation, has risen 688 percent since the enactment of the Great Society programs, Medicare and Medicaid, in 1965.

Mandatory spending, which is not subject to annual review and appropriations, has grown from $180 Billion in 1962 to $1,422 Billion in 2006.

The $2.8 Trillion budget for 2007 projected an additional

$3 Trillion of debt in the next five years.

Federal Spending as a Percentage of GDP Using CBO Baseline, 2000-2050

Since 1962, federal spending has historically consumed 20 percent of GDP. However, the three big entitlement programs -- Medicare, Medicaid, and Social Security -- are projected to explode as baby boomers retire. Even if "Defense" spending and "Other" (non-defense discretionary and small entitlement) spending decline as a share of GDP, rapid growth in the three big entitlements will cause the federal budget to reach 38 percent of GDP. Individual Income Taxes Will Grow Faster than Other Types of Federal Revenue

If federal spending continues on its current steep trajectory, the budget deficit is projected to grow 646 percent by 2050, reaching 19 percent of GDP by 2050 -- well above the historical average of 2.2 percent. Structural deficits at this size -- driven by entitlement spending in Social Security, Medicare, and Medicaid -- have never been seen in the U.S. and illustrate the need to reform these programs.

Spending growth typically increases faster than revenue growth as seen in five of the last eight Administrations.

Federal spending held steady during the 1960's but has increased almost continuously since 1960 regardless of which party controls congressional leadership.

GROWTH OF THE FEDERAL INCOME TAX

The Federal Budget has more than doubled every ten years since 1940. The interest rate on the national debt alone is now more than the entire budget in 1940. The tax burden per person has followed a similar growth pattern. The trend and implications are truly alarming.

The federal income tax represents a prime example of federal expansionism. Its growth closely parallels the growth of the Federal Government. Income taxation was not a power originally granted to the Federal Government by the Constitution. It was added by the 16th Amendment in 1313. It was initially a modest levy with a normal rate of one percent on personal incomes up to $20,000, a surtax up to a maximum of six percent at $500,000 and a flat corporate tax of one percent. It was said. The sole purpose was to raise revenue. Personal exemptions relieved all but the well-to-do from the tax. When one of the legislators objected and suggested that the tax might some day rise to as high as ten percent, he was shouted down as being unrealistic.

The tax has now risen to 35% percent in the highest bracket and a minimum of 10% on first $8,500 of income. 45% pay no income tax at all. Personal exemptions have been drastically reduced and the corporate rate has been increased to thirty five percent, the 3rd highest in the world. The main burden of the tax is now borne by the upper and middle income groups while the high income groups are given little incentive to provide capital for industry and new enterprises. No relief from this burden is in sight and more needs requiring more revenue are being uncovered daily.

The Bush and Obama bailouts and stimulus programs created generational debt obligations that seriously endanger the nation's economic future. It is even more threatening because these debts do not reflect the impact that Social Security and Medicare demands of the Baby Boom generation will have.

The nation is now burdened by many taxes:

Accounts Receivable Tax
Building Permit Tax
CDL license Tax
Cigarette Tax
Corporate Income Tax
Dog License Tax
Federal Income Tax
Federal Unemployment Tax (FUTA)
Fishing License Tax
Food License Tax,
Fuel Permit Tax
Gasoline Tax
Hunting License Tax
Inheritance Tax
Interest expense
Inventory Tax
IRS Interest Charges IRS Penalties (tax on top of tax)
Liquor Tax
Luxury Taxes
Marriage License Tax

Medicare Tax
Property Tax
Real Estate Tax
Service charge taxes
Social Security Tax

State Income Tax
Road usage Taxes
Sales Taxes
Recreational Vehicle Tax
School Tax
State Income Tax
Telephone federal excise tax
Telephone federal universal service fee tax
Telephone federal, state and local surcharge taxes
Telephone minimum usage surcharge tax
Telephone recurring and non-recurring charges tax
Telephone state and local tax
Telephone usage charge tax
Utility Taxes
Vehicle License Registration Tax
Vehicle Sales Tax
Watercraft Registration Tax
Well Permit Tax
Workers Compensation Tax
Etc.

Not one of these taxes existed 100 years ago, and our nation then was the most prosperous in the world. We had absolutely no national debt and had the largest middle class in the world.

LOSS OF MONETARY SIGNIFICANCE

Citizens today have lost a sense of monetary significance, especially when hearing politicians explain spending intentions and facts. Their perceptions of the dimensions and amounts of money actually involved with monetary terms such as; Millions, Billions, or Trillions are often meaningless or unrealistic.

Testing your understanding of Monetary Dimensions

1. What is the largest US $ denomination bill circulated?

2. How many $100 bills make up $1 Million dollars?

3. A Million Dollars equals how many Thousand Dollars?

4. A Billion Dollars equals how many Thousand Dollars?

5. **A Billion Dollars equals how many Million Dollars?**

6. **A Trillion Dollars equals how many Million Dollars?**

7. **A Trillion Dollars equals how many Billion Dollars?**

The term $1 Billion has lost its significance for most Americans. Most people have no real sense of the reality of one Million dollars let alone Billions or Trillions of dollars. State Government budgets now routinely run into the Billions. Federal budgets and the Federal debt are now Trillions of Dollars. Government officials casually discuss and authorize the taxing, distribution and spending of Billion and even Trillion dollar sums.

As one government leader once said, *"A $Billion here and a $Billion there, pretty soon you are talking real money!"*

The term "$ Trillion" has become meaningless. Its use obscures the dangerous nature of national spending, budgets and debts.

Not too long ago, a $ Billion ($ One Thousand Million) as the maximum sum used to describe spending. Even true value of $ One Billion is not clearly understood by most people.

$1 Billion = A stack of $1 bills **75 miles high.**

$1 Trillion = One Thousand Billions.

Politicians should not be allowed to state expenditures in Trillions of Dollars.

For instance in 2011, the Annual Federal Budget was $3 Thousand, 600 Billion Dollars ($3.6 Trillion).

The Annual Federal Budget Deficit (borrowed funds) is

$680 Thousand Million ($680 Billion Dollars).

The Federal Debt is $17+ Thousand Billion Dollars ($17+ Trillion).

State budgets now run in the Billions of dollars and Federal budgets in the Trillions of dollars. Federal budget deficits routinely ran into Hundreds of Billions of dollars even Trillions of dollars.

The 2011 Federal budget was projected to be $3.6 Trillion with a likely deficit of $7 Trillion over the next five years if nothing is changed.

The Power of 1,000

$1 Million = $10,000 $100 dollar bills

$1 Million = $1,000 X 1,000 = $1,000,000

$1 Billion = $1,000,000 X 1,000 = $1,000,000,000

$1 Trillion = $1,000,000,000 X 1000 = $1,000,000,000,000

The Physical Dimensions of Money

$1 Million = A stack of $1 bills **396 Feet high**

$1 Billion = A stack of $1 bills **75 Miles high**

$1 Trillion = A stack of $1 bills **75,000 Miles high or 9.4 times around the world**

$1 BILLION in ½" packages of $10,000 of $100 Bills

$1 Trillion in ½" packages of $10,000 of $100 bills

The next time you hear politicians speak of Billion and Trillion dollar budgets and expenditures, consider the physical dimensions of the money they are spending for a more realistic perspective.

When a politician says he is proposing to spend $1 Billion for a project, ask him if it is worth 1,000 Million Dollars? See if his answer shows that he clearly understands what a Billion Dollars truly represents.

Test Answers:

1. What is the largest US $ denomination bill circulated? A $100 bill.

2. How many $100 bills make up $1 Million dollars? 10,000 $100 bills.

3. A Million Dollars equals how many Thousand Dollars? 1,000.

4. A Billion Dollars equals how many Thousand Dollars? 1,000,000

5. A Billion Dollars equals how many Million Dollars? 1,000

6. A Trillion Dollars equals how many Million Dollars? 1,000,000

7. A Trillion Dollars equals how many Billion Dollars? 1,000

EVALUATIONS AND RE-EVALUATIONS

The great historian of Rome, Theodore Mommsen, when he visited our country more than sixty years ago, was asked what he thought of our country. He replied,

"With more than two thousand years of European experience before your eyes, you have repeated every one of Europe's mistakes. I have no further interest in you."

How many more mistakes have we made during the last sixty years?

Benjamin Franklin was even more pessimistic when he predicted that the Federal Union:

"Can only end in despotism as other forms have done before it when the people shall become so corrupt as to need despotic government, being Incapable of any other."

These are bleak words indeed from these great men, but certainly all who truly love America and understand the principles upon which it was founded must feel a need to strive for a better result. If these principles cannot be made to work, if our people cannot make sound readjustments and maintain effective control of their government, **then there is no governmental system known to mankind that will not eventually be destroyed by its parental society.**

What must be accomplished in our society today is a general, public re-evaluation and re-assessment of the original system of checks and balances, with special consideration being given to why they failed and how they or others which are more effective can be re-established and effectively maintained. A necessary preliminary to such actions would be the accomplishment of a re-awakening of the people to the vital importance of such disciplines in any system of government and to the dangers inherent in any system where they do not exist.

In Article 15 of the Virginia Declaration of Rights, which was drafted by George Mason and adopted in 1776, there appears this statement:

*"No free government or the blessings of liberty can be preserved to any people but by firm adherence to justice, moderation, temperance, frugality, and virtue and by frequent **recurrence to fundamental principles**."* The time for "recurrence to principles" is long overdue.

PART III

CONSERVATIVE SHORT COMINGS - UNPOPULAR PRINCIPLES

The principles on which America was founded can inspire vigorous, positive reactions in people. History has demonstrated that these inspirational concepts are capable of raising people to exceptional heights of endeavor and spirit. And yet, those who promote these concepts, especially in the 2006/08/12 elections have enjoyed very limited successes in terms of political victories. Why is this true? This section will examine recent history with this question in mind. It will suggest some reasons why Conservative/Libertarian viewpoints are not enjoying a more general public acceptance.

The criticisms made herein are intended to be constructive criticisms. Processes of development and growth demand such critical re-examinations. For it is only from such processes that new, better and more successful principles can be created. Libertarians and Conservatives and all who believe in American founding principles and what makes America the greatest nation on earth must enter into such processes. If not, their ideals will face continuing defeats and rejection and they will be ineffective in preventing the eventual end of the American dream.

FREE ENTERPRISE AND THE DEPRESSION

The concepts of freedom for the individual, free enterprise and constitutionally defined checks and balances have been the vigorously pronounced philosophies of Conservatives and Libertarians since the beginning of our country. One cannot disagree with the powerful, incentive creating, productive forces inherent in the application of such philosophies. They are proven in the history of our country leading up to the great depression of 1929. However, it is now generally believed that these philosophies proved themselves to be inadequate as a framework for governing society.

Myths of the Great Depression, by Lawrence W. Reed

How bad was the Great Depression? Over the four years from 1929 to 1933, production at the nation's factories, mines, and utilities fell by more than half. People's real disposable incomes dropped 28 percent. Stock prices collapsed to one-tenth of their pre-crash height. The number of unemployed

Americans rose from 1.6 million in 1929 to 12.8 million in 1933. One of every four workers was out of a job at the Depression's nadir, and ugly rumors of revolt simmered for the first time since the Civil War.

Old myths never die; they just keep showing up in college economics and political science textbooks. Students today are frequently taught that unfettered free enterprise collapsed of its own weight in 1929, paving the way for a decade-long economic depression full of hardship and misery. President Herbert Hoover is presented as an advocate of "hands-off," or laissez-faire, economic policy, while his successor, Franklin Roosevelt, is the economic savior whose policies brought us recovery. This popular account of the Depression belongs in a book of fairy tales and not in a serious discussion of economic history, as a review of the facts demonstrates.

The genesis of the Great Depression lay in the inflationary monetary policies of the U.S. government in the 1920s. It was prolonged and exacerbated by a litany of political missteps: trade-crushing tariffs, incentive-sapping taxes, mind-numbing controls on production and competition, senseless destruction of crops and cattle, and coercive labor laws, to recount just a few. It was not the free market that produced twelve years of agony; rather, it was political bungling on a scale as grand as there ever was.

Regardless of these facts, after continuous liberal propaganda, it is generally believed that the concept of severely limiting the role of the Federal Government paralyzed the government's ability to respond to the disastrous malpractices and manipulations occurring in the stock market and banking system at that time. Free enterprise went out of control and caused the ensuing economic crash. Most Conservatives do not accept or recognize this fact. Nevertheless, this belief does constitute the underlying basic reason for the consistent failure of Conservative or Libertarian philosophies to achieve any substantial degree of public acceptance during subsequent years.

The hardships of the depression years created psychological scars on the minds of the American people. Whether true or not, they have come to believe that free enterprise did run away and create the economic situation that collapsed into the chaos of the depression. Because of this the people feel that some degree of economic control from the federal level is necessary.

FDR recognized this fact and moved in to generate the forces and policies that expanded the role of the Federal Government in seeing to the "general welfare of the nation". His policies of government driven economic and job stimulation failed to end the depression. The requirements of the 2nd World War overrode all economic concerns to meet war efforts and these expenditures finally ended the depression.

During the war, the Federal Government ran budget deficits as high as 28% of Gross Domestic Product (GDP) and the National Debt to over 120% of GDP. Meeting the suppressed demand after the war and a post war reduced Federal Government created a powerful economic recovery which eliminated the deficit by the 1960's and reduced the National Debt to 32% of GDP.

Federal debt almost doubled in the 1980s, reaching 60 percent of GDP in 1990 and peaking at 66 percent of GDP in 1996, before declining to 56 percent in 2001. Federal debt started increasing again in the 2000s, reaching 70 percent of GDP in 2008. Then it exploded in the aftermath of the Crash of 2008, reaching 102 percent of GDP in 2011. Federal debt has breached 100 percent of GDP twice since 1900: during World War II and in the aftermath of the Recession of 2008. It was nearly there in 2012.

POST DEPRESSION

During the period after the depression and prior to Goldwater, the Republican Party definitely aided the growth of the Federal Government in the country. To their credit, the GOP did maintain a stronger insistence on sound management and budgeting practices than their Democratic counterparts. But the basic fact of extensive federal growth did occur and it occurred essentially with little opposition and with significant contributory action by both parties. Predepression conservative philosophy saw only massive public rejection.

Concern over the growing role of the Federal Government gradually began to alarm the people. However, the American history of freedom for the individual began to exert its force on the minds of the people. It was this growing concern that generated the public effort that finally nominated Barry Goldwater as the 1964 Republican candidate for the presidency.

This was the first wide, strong public reaction based on conservative policy since the beginning of the depression. But that policy had one very basic flaw that caused its failure. It was again based on pre-depression conservative philosophy. The people having been persuaded by Liberal, big government promotion were not about to go for these concepts that they believe had failed so disastrously in 1929. Thus, we saw the vigorous rejection of Goldwater and the resultant "mandate" for President Johnson.

ACCEPTANCE OF THIS VIEW

This line of reasoning concerning the failures of the conservative viewpoint over the past 35 years is not widely held nor publicly expounded in any effective manner. However, if such a viewpoint could be accepted by today's Libertarians and Conservatives, a type of thinking would likely develop that would instill new life into a Constitutional Independent philosophy and perhaps achieve a wide re-acceptance for such principles and concepts. Such thinking would take into account a need for greater federal controls than those that are authorized by a strict interpretation of the Congressional Powers and "general welfare" clauses of the Constitution. It would recognize the dangers in this sort of control extension and would establish an enlightened, effective system of checks and balances.

In other words, the goal should be to: *Establish and maintain a responsive, effective government within a free society promoted by a Constitutional Independent philosophy.*

An examination of conservative philosophies that enjoy significant public enunciation and promotion shows a real lack of recognition of the perception, true or not, that free enterprise with limited government failed at the time of the depression. A noteworthy lack is that of a clear recognition that State Governments can no longer provide needed additional governmental services, nor do they effectively serve as checks to federal expansion.

From the depression until Goldwater's campaign in 1964,'the Republican party's public image was one of generally supporting a strong, gradually expanding role for Federal Government in our society with a related deterioration of the state's role. This is what is generally considered to be the strongest image in terms of vote getting and it must be admitted that some election successes were achieved. But the destructive effect to our society in terms of federal expansion over the years is little less than that which would come with unopposed application of liberal Democratic Party principles.

CURRENT CONSERVATISM

Probably the strongest public image of conservatism is that associated with the Goldwater candidacy. This conservative philosophy was defined in a series of articles by Barry Goldwater that were published in the book entitled, "*The Conscience of the Conservative*", in 1960. This image of conservatism is the one that presently enjoys acceptance by most of the people who are amenable to such philosophy. It generally espouses a Libertarian viewpoint with strong concepts of support for individualism in society and a strict interpretation of the Constitution.

Leonard E. Read, President of the "Foundation for Economic Education", defined a basic concept of limited government which well summarizes the role of government in a society according to this viewpoint:

"Government should defend the lives and property of all citizens equally. This means protecting willing exchange and restraining unwilling exchange, suppressing and penalizing fraud, misrepresentation, predatory practices; invoking a common justice under written law; and keeping the records incidental to these functions. Government's legitimate purpose is to codify and then inhibit all destructive actions while leaving all creative and productive actions including welfare, charity, security, and prosperity to citizens acting voluntarily, privately, cooperatively, or competitively, as they freely choose."

INADEQUACIES OF CONSERVATISM

These principles guided America and were tested in our pre-depression society. It was the most vigorous and extensive application of these principles that mankind has ever achieved, but it is generally believed that they failed in the depression. They are perceived as failed because they represent an inadequate set of principles. Inadequate in that they ignore the fact that there are some social and economic problems that demand governmental solutions and controls and some that can only be effectively administered at a national level of government. The strict application of limited government in a free enterprise society freezes the ability of the national government to respond to the problems of a free society that truly demand national solutions.

For example, it took the depression to jar the nation loose from limited government concepts enough to pass the Banking and Securities Acts of 1933 and 1935 and the legislation that created the Federal Deposit Insurance Corporation. The economic stabilization and the confidence in the economy that these controls and support functions generate represent vital influences that have helped our nation achieve the stature it enjoys today. These functions, however, are incompatible with strict conservative concepts of limited government.

THE ROLE OF THE STATES

Another major part of Goldwater conservatism is the promotion of state supremacy in matters of social/economic functions of government. This is a sound concept, for social, welfare and educational functions are undoubtedly best performed at the state or local levels. However, Mr. Goldwater and his conservatives neglected to clearly define a sound program for making the states capable of performing these functions effectively.

To be more explicit, the states have reached tax ceilings. State legislators know that the people are tax saturated. State budgets now run into the Billions of $. They cannot increase taxes to meet the new problems as they arise without encountering powerful opposition. Most states require that their annual budgets must be balanced. The Federal Government, however, is more flexible financially. Through deficit budgeting, printing money and other fiscal maneuvers, and by virtue of the fact it gets the greatest bite of tax dollars, it can and does respond to these national problems.

It is because of this that we saw the gradual shift to what President Johnson called "Creative Federalism". The shift has gone so far that more than 50 percent of the federal budget is now spent on functions that are not clearly authorized in the Constitution. Many of these are more properly state local functions and the trend continues. Mr. Goldwater's platform did promote a proper role for state governments, but he neglected to clearly present a sound, positive, practical program to give them the ability to do it.

The primary problem to be concerned with is one of establishing and maintaining a sound government and economic system within the United States. It is to this end that our strongest efforts should be directed. For, if this nation is internally strong and vigorous, it need never fear international powers. <u>Being internally strong, we would be internationally powerful and by our shining example and success, we would be armored and influential.</u> As our nation adopts and implements policies that provide effective, responsive government within a free society that promotes free market and entrepreneurial principles, societies and people around the world would see our successes and seek to emulate these principles. In other words, concepts of freedom, free enterprise and limited government would be best promoted by our successful example.

Our nation is extremely complex with extensive freedoms of communications, speech and action that allow all expressions of philosophy and sentiment. It must be admitted that today a great portion of government functions at the national level appear to be socialistic in nature.

A PROPOSED CONSTITUTIONAL AMENDMENT

Among conservatives, there is one group that is active in promoting a specific program for re-establishing a clear positive, state favored balance between the State and Federal Governments. The "Liberty Amendment Committee of the USA" is committed to the education of the public in this matter. This group supports the passage of what they have named, "The Liberty Amendment" for the Constitution of the United States. Following is a text of the proposed amendment and a summary statement taken from a supporting book titled, "Action far Americans - The Liberty Amendment" by Lloyd G. Herbstreith and Gordon Van B. King:

THE LIBERTY AMENDMENT

Section 1.   The Government of the United States shall not engage in any business, commercial, financial or industrial enterprise except as specified in the Constitution.

Section 2. The Constitution or laws of any State, or the laws of the United States, shall not be subject to the terms of any foreign or domestic agreement that would abrogate this amendment.

Section 3.   The activities of the United States Government that violate the intent and purposes of the amendment shall, within a period of three years from the date of ratification of this amendment, be liquidated and the properties and facilities affected shall be sold.

Section 4. Three years after the ratification of this amendment, the sixteenth article of amendments to the Constitution of the United States shall stand repealed and thereafter Congress shall not levy taxes on personal incomes, estates, and or gifts.

SUMMARY STATEMENT

"THE: LIBERTY AMENDMENT, which was introduced into Congress by the Hon. James B. Utt, of California, is pending as House Joint Resolution 23. It is simultaneously being introduced before the Legislatures of the Several States with the intent of obtaining identical resolutions approving it".

"THE LIBERTY AMENDMENT is a proposed Amendment to the Constitution of the United States. It will not change the spirit and intent of the original Constitution. It will merely clarify it, to give it force and effectiveness".

"The Liberty Amendment states that the Federal Government shall not operate business type activities unless they are specifically authorized by the Constitution. It provides a three-year period for selling or liquidating the more than 700 business-type enterprises presently operated by the Government without constitutional authority. Sale of these enterprises will bring in enough money to reduce the national debt by at least twenty percent. Annual budget spending by the Government will be reduced by more than fifty percent. Revenue from excise taxes on goods and services, and on corporation incomes, will increase at least twenty percent, without increase of tax rates".

"This means that the annual revenue collected from the Federal Personal Income and Withholding Tax, the Federal Estate Tax, and the Federal Gift Tax will not be needed. So the Liberty Amendment will stop these three types of taxes, at the end of the three-year period".

"The Liberty Amendment was originally known as the Proposed 23rd Amendment. However, in 1961, a proposal to allow voting in the District of Columbia was ratified, and became the 23rd Amendment. rather than calling our proposal the "24th Amendment", it has been re-named the Liberty Amendment, to identify it better and to connect it with its true purpose; To re-establish personal liberty under constitutional government.*"*

LIMITED SUCCESS

Wide public knowledge or this effort does not exist. This is somewhat remarkable in that the development of the amendment began in 1944 and, since 1959, it has been promoted on a national level as well as through the state legislatures. The proponents or this amendment are still actively pursuing its passage.

The Liberty Amendment has progressed toward ratification to a degree not widely known by the public. Nine states have endorsed the Liberty Amendment by passing the necessary resolutions requesting the amendment be submitted to the states for ratification. The endorsement in nearly all state legislatures was bi-partisan and close to unanimous.

These states are:

Wyoming · Nevada · Texas · Louisiana · Georgia · South Carolina · Mississippi · Arizona · Indiana

If the amendment were passed as proposed, the role of the Federal Government in the economy would be strictly limited to constitutionally defined powers and the states would be able to reestablish a strong role in providing social, welfare and educational functions. This would represent a much more satisfactory alternative to the present trend toward centralization and excessive federal control. But because of the drastic nature of its implementation and the lack of recognition given to needed federal economic/social functions it is likely that the amendment as proposed will never be enacted.

Once again, this amendment will not gain wide public support because, in essence, it establishes a pre-depression form of government. The public, remembering the damaging depression era, will insist on some degrees of federal control in the social/economic environment of the nation.

An even more unacceptable aspect of the "Liberty Amendment" is the proposal that the transition in government would be accomplished over a period of three years. This would be a much too rapid and drastic change and would be totally unacceptable to most people. The practicality of eliminating over fifty percent of the federal functions with the related shifts in spending power over a 3 year period would be unacceptable to most of the general public.

Once again, the people are presented, with two extremely opposite alternatives. On the one hand, they have the seemingly present security of the "greater governmental philosophies" and on the other, a proposal for abrupt national upheaval and a return to a form of government that they believe failed at the time of the depression. The resultant choice would seem to be obvious.

Democratic societies seldom change their basic forms of government in drastic, abrupt ways. It has been said that seldom is liberty lost all at once.

Adjustments to better, free government should also be made slowly and peacefully. Changes in direction can be accomplished and gradual pursuit of new directions can be successfully implemented. The Fabian Socialists recognized this and, through a "creeping socialism" have extended their influences throughout the free world. If Libertarian philosophies are to gain strength again it will probably be through gradual processes following a redirection of national constitutional policy.

REAGAN CONSERVATISM

The conservative principles that have the greatest acceptance today among moderate and conservative Republicans alike are similar to those advocated by President Reagan. Having started his political career as a New Deal Democrat, after joining the Goldwater candidacy he promoted a new, pragmatic blend of political philosophy seeing excess government as an enemy of American principles along with a positive image of America as "a shining city on a hill". He was a conservative reformist who was fond of Tom Paine's adage, *"We have it in our power to begin the world over again."*

The fundamental fact about Reagan's conservatism is not just that it is Conservatism but that it is also patriotic and positive. Reaganism has survived and is strongly supported by the Republican Party because it goes with the grain of American culture. It taps into many of the deepest sentiments in American life; freedom, religiosity, capitalism, patriotism, individualism and optimism.

After Reagan, during Bush Presidencies, the Republican Party became more and more accepting of an expanding role for the Federal Government. With the terrorist destruction of the Trade Towers in New York in 2001, a justification for War On Terror expansion of Homeland bureaucracies and Defense spending was created. The Iraq and Afghanistan wars were started leading to more than a decade of loss of life and financial expenditure with little real accomplishment for American interests.

Lack of regulation played a part in bringing about a major recession that began in 2007 and continues in the slowest recovery since the World War II. There were no regulations that stopped the financial and banking institutions from creating the credit swap and elaborate mortgage exchange systems that became the "toxic assets" mess that caused the recession to be so severe.

The "toxic assets'" were the defective mortgages given to unqualified buyers that were encouraged by Federal Government policies implemented through the mortgage management programs "Freddy and Fanny". When these bad mortgages were distributed throughout the financial and banking systems and defaults began, the entire, world, financial systems were affected. Presidents Bush and Obama used unprecedented bail out expenditures to counteract financial impacts and stimulate the economy.

The 2012 Presidential Election

The Reelection of President Obama gave him the ability to: Fully implement the Affordable Health Care law (Obama Care). If completely installed it will become a permanent National Universal Health Care Institution, National Socialized Medicine.

He will be able to appoint two or more Supreme Court justices. ensuring Progressive (Liberal) support for constitutional rulings.

If he is able to pass an Immigration Law with amnesty for 11+ Million Hispanic voters who will add to the Democratic base of minorities, government service beneficiaries, unions and government workers. It will also encourage more illegal immigration.

The effect will be to make it very difficult for Republicans to win elections.

PART IV

REVITALIZATION: A FEDERAL / STATE BALANCE - ESSENTIAL

If an effective alternative is to be developed to oppose the trend to excessive federalism, the role of the states and localities must be revitalized so that they can effectively respond to new problems and so that welfare, social and educational functions can be returned to them. It is hypocritical to hear present day politicians expounding the notion that the problems that arise should be handled by the states and that the states are neglectful in not assuming these duties. The states do not have access to the additional financial resources that would be needed to make them truly responsive. This lack on the part of the states must be recognized as the primary reason that we see an expanding federacy in the social/economic environment of this nation.

Recently, some national leaders have been providing an answer to state tax problems in which the Federal Government makes direct mandates and tax "rebates or grants" to the states. Some mandates are made without supporting grants. This still represents a usurpation of state taxing powers. Federal controls and Influences come with any money so provided. The federal legislators would be remiss in their duties if they did not insist on some controls, if not initially, then gradually. So the federal growth process continues. The people lose by the delays and ineffective applications that must be inherent in such a system. Certainly such money is considerably devalued by the time it was returned to the states and put to useful purpose. Clearly, the proper approach is to keep the tax money where it will be used in the first place where and whenever possible.

Decentralization and democracy, these are imperatives in any form of government that would, hope to achieve and retain a healthy balance of freedom and effective responsiveness. Democracy is heavily promoted in our nation which is constitutionally defined as a Republic. Very little, however, is heard about the importance of decentralization though this concept is heavily stressed in our constitution.

Felix Morley stated;

"Indeed one of the great virtues of Federalism is the power given to constituent units (states) *to adopt experimental measures in accordance with the wishes of local majorities, without imposing such developments on sections not ready or willing to go along. Political democracy is thus localized*

or qualified but in no sense denied under the American system."

NEW CONCEPTS OF GOVERNMENT

Constitutional Independence suggests ways to accomplish a "recurrence to constitutional principles" thereby returning constitutional rights to the people and providing for a government that is constitutional, effective and yet responsive to the nation's needs and restoring liberty to the individual, dignity to the legislature and purpose to the ballot box.

Constitutional Independents must seek out, promote and support national leaders who will advocate not only duties of the people but also functional checks and balances for government. These must be leaders who will insist that equality consists not of equal, imposed condition but of an equal right for individuals to compete with others under the American system to achieve their full potential. These must be those who will insist that government must become, once again, truly constitutional whether this means an update of the constitution or an update of governmental structures, probably both. They must establish a meaningful system of control for our Federal Government. For, as things exist now, our national government is on a dangerous path of essentially limitless extension and expansion. A dangerous situation indeed for God like wisdom is needed to properly exercise unlimited power.

The creative imagination and energies of Constitutional Independents and all concerned Americans must be brought to bear on these problems. Ways must be found to define and promote the role of effective, responsive government in a free society. Such government:

1. Must be efficiently responsive to valid functional needs at both the state and federal levels.

2. It must establish and retain efficient functions at the lowest appropriate level of control.

3. It must be self-disciplining with effective oversight, operational checks and balances.

4. It must possess effective processes of periodic function review, rejustification and adjustment.

5. Its functions must be Constitutionally authorized, responsible and controlled.

EFFECTIVE, RESPONSIVE GOVERNMENT

The inability of the Federal Government to effectively control illegal immigration shows how politics and bureaucracies influenced by pressure groups make effective immigration policies difficult to implement. Democrats are reluctant to really stop illegal immigration because, with amnesty, they see potential Democratic voters.

Republicans do not act on illegal immigration because of the business influence that likes the cheap labor. Border walls proposed are simply token efforts that cannot effectively control thousands of miles of border. Even if built, such lengthy walls will be climbed over or under and breached when patrols are unable to stop them.

The most effective solution to the illegal immigration problem is to eliminate the illegal immigrant job magnet by providing employers the means to accurately identify illegal employees and to penalize businesses that still knowingly hire illegal aliens.

By eliminating immigrant job potentials and any support systems that encourage them, they will return to their country and, if interested, will choose to utilize legal immigration processes to come to America and become legitimate citizens.

The response of government at all levels to the Katrina flooding disasters clearly showed how ineffective government bureaucracies are at all levels. These responses showed how indecision and improper help occurred at all levels from city to state to the Federal Government. Decisions were slow in coming and confused in implementation. Buck passing and an inability to determine responsibilities were common and caused many response problems.

A government that is truly responsive is one that will react in a prompt, effective manner to new problems that arise. By remaining financially and operationally efficient, it will be capable of such response. To remain efficient implies the existence of continual, viable, active processes of functional oversight, renewal, adjustment and elimination. Efficiency can only come with a high degree of control and intelligent control can only come through a close relationship with the people governed. These are delicate, fragile relationships that can easily be destroyed as has been shown by history.

A concept of effective government represents a philosophy that can be politically successful because it is positive and appeals to mankind's reasoning power. What is truly lacking as an alternative to "greater government" concepts is a reasoned approach to the use of federal powers. Such an approach would give full recognition to the fact that certain federal social / economic functions are necessary. At the same time; it would recognize the fact that whenever such functions are necessary and are established, they represent a great danger and must be subjected to extra special controls and disciplines to ensure that they continue to remain appropriate and necessary functions at the federal level.

LAW IN A FREE SOCTETY

The application of law in welfare, social or educational matters is extremely dangerous as was explained by the French statesman and economist Fredrick Bastiat over 100 years ago to the people of France. At that time in his book "The Law", he told them:

"If you attempt to make the law religious, fraternal, equalizing, philanthropic, industrial, literary or artistic - you will then be lost in an uncharted territory, in vagueness and uncertainty, in a forced utopia or, even worse, in a multitude of utopias, each trying to seize the law and impose it upon you. This is true because fraternity and philanthropy, unlike justice, do not have precise limits. Once

started, where will you stop and where will the law stop itself?"

Fredrick Bastiat also recommended a method of judging whether a law is a good law or a bad law. He said:

"See if the law takes from some persons what belongs to them and gives it to other persons to whom it does not belong ... Then abolish this law without delay, for it is not only an evil itself, but also it is a fertile source for further evils because it invites reprisals. If such a law - which may be only an isolated, case - is not abolished immediately, it will spread, multiply and develop into a system."

The truths in these words are clearly proven by any evaluation of the world's societies today. In America we have used the law in every way he tells us not to. The French people obviously ignored his advice and history proves again and again that people will not restrict their laws in the ways he suggests. His advice is highly idealistic.

So realistic Constitutional Independents, instead, of strictly advocating Bastiat's idealism, should assume the role of educators who will sensitize the people to the dangers in the use of the law and advocate the creation of disciplines that will ensure that dangerous uses must be subject to critical, effective controls and management. Thus, their attitudes toward new needed legislation, especially at the state and local levels, can be effective and positive and they can be recognized as being proponents of reason and moderation in government. Without such an image, their philosophies cannot hope to be politically successful.

Constitutional Independents, in expounding on the merits of free enterprise, should also remember the oligopolistic corporate structures within our society and, in this respect, develop and promote vigorous regulatory policies that will enhance and sustain an environment where free enterprise will thrive and where profiteering abuses will be restricted. A lack of governmental response in establishing such regulatory policies during the period prior to the depression is seen as a principle contributory factor to the crash. Not to be overlooked is the fact that there is great voter attraction in such policies. They are basic to a free concept of society and the reluctance of conservatives to vigorously promote them must be overcome. Government, especially at the national level should not be limited in this respect.

CONSERVATISM

The term "Conservatism" itself has come to have an especially negative connotation during recent years. The general public equates this term with right wing and, too often, with radicalism or obstructive philosophies.

Roget's International Thesaurus lists the following as being synonymous with "Conservative": *"Unprogressive, reactionary, rightist, right winger, die hard, bitter ender, stand patter, uncompromiser, irreconcilable, intransigent, old fogey, stick in the mud, moss back, hard shell, long hair and, old school."*

These are hardly proper words to use to describe positive American philosophies of freedom. Yet the strongest advocates of basic American principles proudly proclaim the fact they are "Conservatives". They glory in this negative term and then wonder why their propositions do not find wide acceptance. This term should be shunned by all who would advance principles of freedom and sound American government.

The accepted alternative to the term Conservative is Liberal. Synonymous with Liberal is: *progressive, reactionary, open-minded, generous, broad-minded, moderate, free-thinking, tolerant, progressive, protective, etc.*

The term Liberal has lost favor recently. So the term Progressive is now used more commonly to describe what Liberal used to mean. Progressive is equally definitive of a bias to larger government influences.

Essentially, the principles of constitutionality, freedom and balanced government are Constitutional Independent principles. Let us hear not only of libertarian concepts in relationship to civil liberties. Liberty is preserved through an observance of Constitutional Independent principles relative to all functions of government and all individual rights.

Often the term "Conservative" is attached as a derogatory label by Liberals. Those who would promote a positive Constitutional Independent view point would be wise to be alert for such labeling tactics and expose them for what they are when encountered. Suggest that such a view point is really a "Constitutional Independent" view point. Positive terms should be substituted wherever possible in dialogues such as: constructive, effective, responsive, reasoned, moderate, center, effective, American, independent, etc.

The obstructive battle to prevent new legislation is one that enjoys little success because usually the current needs that inspired the proposals are real and possess vital strength. So if conservatives focus their energies against such efforts they will attain and deserve the negative image that develops. Battles against legislation which expands existing government can be much more fruitful because such legislation usually does not possess the sound supporting reasoning that initial legislation does. Also, responsive support of necessary new legislation that fills a real need helps develop a positive image that is essential to consistently win elections. Consistent winning of democratic elections is of course, fundamental to the success of any governmental philosophy.

PART V:

SOLUTIONS

There is a great deal of conservative literature available which, through critical analysis, defines the error of our ways and describes what societies would be like if the people and the Federal Government were faithful to Constitutional government. Seldom though, do the authors of this literature propose reasonable, specific actions that can be taken. Usually, they end their exhortations with an appeal for an education of the people that, supposedly, will save the society. History tells us how successful these methods have been. We cannot expect education to return the people to Constitutional principles once they are as far down the road to socialistic over-government and acceptance of dependent services as we are today.

Part of the reason for this inability to reform governmental institutions is that the supporters of "Greater Government" are also conducting massive educational campaigns to condition the people for further acceptance of dependent services and securities. These advocates are well funded. With promises of solutions to problems and more for everyone, they develop highly effective campaigns of persuasion. Endless studies ingeniously contrive to provide "new sources of revenue" which are derived from the only true source, the tax-payer-consumer. The tax - spend - elect cycle seems infinitely productive of "Greater Government". Libertarian advocates of conservative austerity have had, and always will have, a difficult time being educationally successful in such a political climate.

Today, the best known proponent of Libertarian Politics is Texas Representative, Ron Paul. These are some of his recommendations for a more Libertarian Federal Government:

* Veto any unbalanced budget Congress sends to his desk.

* Refuse to further raise the debt ceiling so politicians can no longer spend recklessly.

* Fight to fully audit (and then end) the Federal Reserve System which has enabled the over 95% reduction of what our dollar can buy and continues to create money out of thin air to finance future debt.

* Legalize sound money, so the government is forced to get serious about the dollar's value.

* End the corporate stranglehold on the White House.

* Drive down gas prices by allowing offshore drilling, abolishing highway motor fuel taxes, increasing the mileage reimbursement rates, and offering tax credits to individuals and businesses for the use and production of natural gas vehicles.

* Eliminate the income, capital gains, and death taxes to ensure you keep more of your hard-earned money and are able to pass on your legacy to your family without government interference.

* Oppose all unfunded mandates and unnecessary regulations on small businesses and entrepreneurs.

The Libertarian policies of Ron Paul were discussed during the primary debates where he was a candidate for the Republican ticket. He had a growing group of supporters but far less than were needed to seriously impact Democrat or Republican policies. His policy influences will be very important if Federal Government fiscal policies finally lead to insolvency. His son Rand Paul continues to promote these principles which finds considerable acceptance especially with younger citizens.

Libertarian educational processes should continue to be promoted. This must be done because these processes will reach many of the activists in political life. These activists are relatively few in number but they are the effective means of actual political accomplishment. Libertarian activists, however, must be given reasonable, attractive programs to promote. The primary reason that Libertarians have such limited success is because they only promote freedom from government programs and offer no new benefits. This constitutes the great lack in our society today; reasonable, salable alternatives to the programs of "Greater Government", a "Constitutional Independent" philosophy.

It is suggested that here is a frontier of thought and creative need that waits unfulfilled. It is the area of the political spectrum between the Conservative/Libertarian right and the Liberal/Progressive left. It is the task of defining the nature and method of government that is effective, self-disciplining and free. It demands studies and ideas that will discipline over-extensions of government and at the same time free improperly used governmental resources to reduce government or respond effectively to society's valid needs. It requires definitions of techniques of review and re-justification that can be applied to uproot and prevent stagnation and bureaucratic entrenchment and expansion. It requires concepts that will identify, minimize and dissolve despotic power structures within our society.

Actions and programs must be developed based on historical perspectives not only on transient deficiencies and needs in our nation today. With a historical viewpoint that soundly considers proven, effective concepts and carefully avoids clear errors, techniques can be devised that will allow a continuing **"recurrence to constitutional principle"**.

This is a challenge for Americans today. A problem cannot be resolved until sufficient symptoms exist to define it. Today we have an abundance of symptoms and the errors of our ways can be clearly defined. The demand for action is squarely up to us today. We must choose elected leaders who will guide us in a response to this challenge. Educators and students should be especially responsive to these creative needs and studies. Columnists, editorialists and all persons in a position to influence public opinion must help. For if we do not act, if we continue to drift and decay under concepts of "Greater Government", history must judge the fault to be our own.

THE GENERAL WELFARE CLAUSE

The "General Welfare" clause in the Constitution which has been interpreted to authorize the present federal actions in welfare, social, business and educational matters is in a general statement at the beginning of Section R of the Constitution; Article I, Section R of the Constitution begins:

"The Congress shall have power to levy and collect taxes, duties, imposts and excises, to pay the debts and provide for the common defense and general welfare of the United States; but all duties, imposts and excises shall be uniform throughout the States.

Section F3 continues on for 17 paragraphs to delegate specific powers to Congress;

To borrow money on the credit of the United States. To regulate commerce with foreign nations and among the States and with the Indian tribes. To establish a rule of naturalization and uniform laws on bankruptcies. To coin money, regulate the value thereof and fix the standard of weights and measures. To provide for the punishment of counterfeiting. To establish post offices. To promote science and useful arts by securing exclusive rights to their writing and discoveries. To constitute tribunals inferior to the Supreme court. To punish piracies on the high seas and offences against the laws Of nations. To declare war. To raise and support armies. To provide and maintain a navy. To make rules for land and naval forces. To provide for calling forth the militia. To provide for organizing the militia. To exercise legislation over such district forts, arsenals, and other needful buildings.

Paragraph 18 states; *To make all laws which shall be necessary and proper for carrying into execution the foregoing powers and all other powers vested by this Constitution in the government of the United. States, or in any department or officer thereof.*

It is clearly evident that none of these Constitutional definitions now authorize the vast social and economic functions our Federal Government performs today. The prevalent liberal interpretation takes the words "provide for the general welfare" as a blanket, constitutional, authority for the Federal Government to initiate and carry out any function that the Congress may decide on as being for the general welfare of the nation.

The **Commerce Clause** is an enumerated power listed in the United States Constitution.

(Article I, Section 8, Clause 3). *The clause states that the United States Congress shall have power To regulate Commerce with foreign Nations, and among the several States, and with the Indian Tribes.*

This Clause is also used to justify expansive uses of Federal power.

These interpretations are taken in direct contradiction to the abundance of language in the Constitution which restricts the role of the Federal Government in the society, especially in social/economic matters. It implies a disregard for the intent expressed in the Bill of Rights in the Ninth Amendment:

"The enumeration in the Constitution of certain rights shall not be construed to deny or disparage others retained by the people."

and in the Tenth Amendment:

"The powers not delegated to the United States by the Constitution, nor prohibited by it to the States, are reserved to the States respectively, or to the people".

This disregard for the restrictive clauses in the Constitution has been allowed since the 1930's. It is likely that the people have allowed this interpretation to take effect because they were reacting to the crushing effects of the depression. They sensed a need for more federal power and flexibility and therefore concurred. After some 80 years of experience with this interpretation, however, it is clear that some reevaluation, **"recurrence to constitutional principle"** is required.

The Federal Government has exceeded reasonable restraints and gives every indication of being capable of endlessly growing and accumulating and centralizing power of all kinds. Perhaps becoming **"Too Big To Survive"**.

If the national debt is to be brought under control, limits must be established on federal government expansion.

We see many of the reasonable powers of the states being gradually usurped by the Federal Government. These extensive power assumptions must be brought under a more definitive control, preferably a constitutional control. If the Constitution is to represent any sort of meaningful guide for governing this nation, clarification of the "General Welfare" clause is required.

One way to restrain Federal spending would be to repeal the 16th Amendment that authorizes the Federal income tax. The repeal could probably never be accomplished, but the process of the states going through the process of attempting the repeal would definitely send a clear message to the Federal Government that it must restrain its exorbitant fiscal ways. This would only be a temporary influence on government and in time big spending would likely resume. Something more permanent and more acceptable is what is needed.

Today, most American citizens seem to generally agree that the Federal Government should be involved in many areas that do not find specific authorization in the Constitution. The "General Welfare" and "Commerce" clauses can be, and in fact has been, liberally construed to authorize federal activities in almost any field. This has been established in precedent activity and by consensus approval at the polls. Indeed, reasonable thought must find logic in the concept that a national constitution cannot specifically define all the powers of a Federal Government. Still, dangerous centralization of governmental power can take place and, in fact, has already taken place.

What is needed is an authorization that would, allow the Federal Government to move in where national problems exist but one which would preserve a practical amount of oversight and control as well as decentralization through retention of adequate state and local governmental powers. One way in which this could be accomplished would be through an amendment to the Constitution which would allow the states to establish a maximum limit on total federal expenditures/budgets.

AN EXAMPLE AMENDMENT

An example draft of a constitutional amendment would help to demonstrate some techniques that would establish some of the governmental disciplines that have been previously discussed and stimulate further considerations that might lead to ideal solutions.

This example amendment would be aimed at correcting that basic defect in the Constitution that is proposed to be corrected by the "Liberty Amendment", specifically, the "General Welfare" clause.

An amendment is here proposed to rectify the dangerous course of our national government and reestablish Constitutional significance. Granted, this amendment would represent a major change in the role of the States relative to the Federal Government. Such strengthening of state influences would be needed if the Federal Government continues to demonstrate continuing inability to effectively manage the nation's fiscal responsibilities.

A FEDERAL LIMIT AMENDMENT

The total annual expenditures of the Federal Government of the United States shall not exceed a limit established at the time of ratification of this amendment except as may be authorized at any time for periods of up to twelve months by at least fifty one percent of the State Legislatures. After ratification of this amendment, all income of the Federal Government of the United States in excess of the established expenditure limit shall be disbursed to the States on the basis of population or shall be used to reduce the national debt.

The states, in initial agreement, designed, created and ratified the Constitution of the United States. Ultimately the states must concur in the validity of the US Constitution. If the Federal Government significantly deviates from the specifications in the Constitution, Article 5 defines the right of states to propose and ratify amendments as needed.

Amendment ratification by ¾ of the several States or by conventions

Ratification of a Federal Limit Amendment would require approval of three fourths of the State Legislatures. **The states would be in favor of such an amendment because of the greater influence they would obtain over growth of the Federal Government and the potential of getting surplus funds.** State's rights and constitutional federalism would be reinforced. This fact would provide a strong incentive for states to use their founding powers and constitutional right to institute a Federal Limit Amendment.

The 26th amendment (granting the right to vote for 18 year-olds) took only 3 months & 8 days to be ratified! Why? The people demanded it. That was in 1971 before computers, e-mail, cell phones, etc. Of the 27 amendments to the Constitution, seven (7) took 1 year or less to become the law of the land all because of public pressure.

Ratification can also be accomplished through a Constitutional Convention that can be called by two thirds of both houses of Congress or two thirds of the State Legislatures. To make an almost painless transition, the federal limit could be set at the amount of the Federal Budget as of the time of ratification. Thus, its approval would represent no abrupt national upheaval but would constitute a definite act of re-direction that would immediately go into effect.

Basic effects:

Basic disciplines would be created by such an amendment;

1. Control of the size and growth of the Federal Government through constitutional budgetary restraints.

2. Debt reduction or dispersion of excess federal funds in a manner that is nationally equitable and not subject to federal political influence.

3. Federal competition for available funds within the limit will increase program oversight, rejustification and the reduction and elimination of unnecessary functions.

4. State competition for available funds would add an additional check and balance effect to the Federal Government.

5. The Constitutional Congressional requirement to declare war would be reinforced. The Vietnam, Iraq and Afghanistan wars would likely not have been authorized and funded with this amendment in effect.

6. States rights and constitutional federalism would be strengthened. This fact would provide a strong incentive for states to use their constitutional right to institute a Federal Limit Amendment.

TOTAL EXPENDITURES CONTROLLED

Note that the total expenditures of the Federal Government would be limited. This would have to include all its functions; defense as well as non-defense spending including what are called discretionary and non-discretionary expenditures. All Federal disbursements must be covered by this limit to ensure that no unauthorized growth can develop. No off budget authorizations can be allowed. The primary reason for such an amendment would be to reestablish a Constitutional Federal Government.

To be effective, such fiscal control must be complete.

While totality of control would have to be affected, it would not be an inflexible control. A simple majority of the State Legislatures could authorize a change in the federal expenditures limit at any time. Such a change would remain in effect for up to twelve months. It is conceivable that a limit expansion would come to be annually re-authorized and carried along year after year. This could occur when a popular expansionist consensus develops and is sustained in a majority of the states. An annual review and renewal on the part of the states would be required but this would certainly be a limit authorization exercise that would ensure a continuing proper role for the Federal Government in relation to the states in the nation.

Serious threats that can be clearly defined such as imminent war or national disaster would certainly stimulate a prompt response for a limit change from a majority of the states if needed. Such clear dangers would easily retain the necessary support and annual limit re-approval. The national administration would have to clearly present the case and move the states to action when dangers threaten national security that will demand resources beyond the budget limit. Indefinite, unclear declarations of national danger would probably find difficulty in getting support in the national budget. Sustaining support for such pseudo threats would he almost impossible to sustain for any significant period of time.

The Constitution was originally authorized by the states of the union. It is the founding power and ratification by the States of America that ultimately give the Federal Government its powers through the Constitution. When it exceeds these powers beyond reason, the states have the constitutional right and duty though amendment to correct any such abuses. This Federal Limit Amendment sets up a subtle but powerful competition for government revenues between the states and within the Federal Government that is flexible in execution and free from inappropriate political influences.

BUDGETARY DISCIPLINES

The concept of using budgetary disciplines and processes to establish fiscal control and administrative management within the Federal Government gave birth to Bureau of the Budget through the Budget and Accounting Act of 1921. The bureau this act created prepares an integrated plan of financial estimates and has specific authority to make studies of the organizations and operations of the executive branch.

The Director and Deputy Director of the Budget are appointed by the President without Senate confirmation. The Budget and Accounting Act of 1921 also laid the legal Framework for unified control over departmental accounts and for a government wide audit system and budget formation in these areas:

The military, commerce and finance, labor and welfare, and resources and civil works legislative reference, management and organization of the executive branch, statistical standard definition and implementation and financial management procedures for all bureaus and departments.

The federal budget process begins at the spring of each year. Overall budgetary policy is defined at the cabinet level. These policies are then disseminated with guidelines and a call for estimates and definitions of intended agency programs. This call is over 12 months in advance of the relevant fiscal year that begins July 1st.

Within each agency, the budget officers obtain estimates from the bureaus and divisions. These estimates are extensively reviewed and examined within the agencies before being submitted to the Budget Bureau examiners. Hearings are then held for the individual Agencies to allow them to defend and clarify proposals and budget requirements. From these hearings and examinations, recommendations are drafted and submitted for approval to the Budget Director and his review groups. After approval by the Director has been obtained, the estimates and highlights of each agency's requirements are submitted to the President for his approval.

At the beginning of the legislative session which begins in January, the President presents the budget prepared by this process in a budget message and by reports to the Congress and the nation. Committees of the Congress review this "Presidential Budget" and Congress, provides guidance in the preparation of appropriation proposals. When these proposals are passed by the Congress, they represent the "Appropriations Act" for that year. The Bureau of the Budget then becomes involved in enforcing the budgetary disciplines imposed by the "Appropriations Act" through out the federal agencies.

It is an indication of how the Federal Government has lost effective control of its fiscal condition in that the Senate has failed to pass a budget in over 3 years.

An extensive apparatus exists for governmental cost estimation, review, justification, fiscal procedure and functional audit in the federal budget system. If this system has failed to act as a viable controlling force in government, and federal growth patterns in recent decades would indicate that this is true, it is probably because the Bureau of the Budget is not an unbiased part of the federal power structure. Its purpose is to provide financial analysis of pending legislation and existing services. Indeed, reason would say that, by its nature and function in the federal legislative system, the bureau's biases would have supported the excessive growth patterns.

The Budget Bureau's expertise, methods and system could probably be more effective in a federal environment where, because of constitutionally defined fiscal limits, agencies must compete for available funds. Its audit and accounting systems could be a great aid in locating departments and functions which are weak and not supportable among prevailing priorities. The bureau's broad authorities and review procedures could be a powerful catalyst in the process of governmental discipline and rejuvenation. It could be the communicative and examining force that would help make agency and departmental competition work. Given the incentive of a constitutionally enforced spending limit, the budget system could be more effective in the performance of these vital disciplinary services. For instance, here is an excerpt from the 2012 Annual GAO Report...

The Federal Government Accountability Office GAO 2012 annual report addresses duplication and areas for costs savings throughout the federal government; The 2012 GAO duplication report reviewed 51 areas of government spending, including 32 areas of extensive federal duplication, fragmentation and overlap, and 19 areas for large cost savings through addressing waste and mismanagement. And like last year's report, which identified more than $100 billion in budgetary savings by simply eliminating duplicative programs, today's findings are a testament to failed congressional efforts of oversight and a reminder Congress continue to shirk its duty to address even blatant areas of waste and mismanagement of taxpayer funding. Duplication exists throughout every federal agency and every corner of the budget, from the Department of Defense, to special interest tax *credits, and every federal agency and office on Constitution Avenue. The problem in Congress today is not an issue of ignorance. It is one of indifference and incompetence .*

LIMIT ADEQUACY

How large should the federal sector of government be in our society? There is almost certainly no fixable limit that is proper for all time. Probably as of today, it is too large. Far too many of the present federal functions should be state functions or should be eliminated, reduced or replaced with different, better programs of action at the state and local levels.

It is conceivable that with the passage of an amendment such as the Federal Limit Amendment, the role of the government could be effectively reduced. On the other hand, perhaps not. Perhaps the role of the Federal Government would have to be increased even beyond its present size when the society continues to grow and require more national services. The important thing is that either growth or contraction can occur under constitutional control and a mechanism would exist with a Federal Limit Amendment by which effective control of these processes could be maintained.

USE OF EXCESS FEDERAL FUNDS

A key effect such a limit amendment would have would be to create a reflective ceiling for federal funds. It would be reflective in that it would force dispersion of excess funds collected downward to lower levels of government based on population. Thus, states and, through the states, local governmental units would receive funds free of requirements to enable them to be responsive to the problems and needs of the people.

If the federal expenditures ceiling were fixed at the level as of the time of amendment ratification, no immediate funds would be available for dispersion. But with continuing growth in the nation's economy and with income tax rates continuing at the same level, the federal income from taxes would exceed the expenditures limit. This excess income would then become funds dispersible to the states. The amendment would require that these excess funds be utilized either by allocation to the states on the basis of population or for reduction of the national debt. The Federal Government's only discretionary power regarding such funds would be to decide whether the funds should be given to the states or used to reduce the Federal debt. Of course, the Federal Government would still retain the power to raise or lower taxes as a means of controlling economic cash flow increase or reduction to counteract major inflationary or recessionary trends.

Because the powers of the Federal Government would be limited in this respect, funds allocated to the states could be funds free of federal controls. Thus, effective decentralization of government could be accomplished. On the other hand, the Federal Government would have a strong reason for using the funds to control the national debt effectively. Since the funds could not be used to expand federal powers, the government could be relatively unbiased in its use of such excess funds.

A powerful, safe tool would be provided to deal with problems of the national economy. In times of recession, the Federal Government could choose to disperse excess income downward to the states thereby stimulating the economy. It may even choose to augment these funds with borrowed funds to create greater impacts. It is important to note that, through the states and local governments the spending would be decentralized and thus more effectively done than would be possible through Washington. In times of inflation, the government could choose to levy taxes to dampen inflationary pressures. In this case, the income from such taxes would be used to reduce the national debt. It could not be used to increase federal functions. In either case, federal growth would be appropriately restricted.

A SIMPLE, REASONABLE STEP

Most importantly, ratification of such a Federal Limit Amendment would represent a relatively simple step toward control establishment that would not demand a drastic deviation from existing governmental policies and governmental functions. It is possible that the limit established at the time of the Constitutional Convention could be set equal to the amount of the prevailing total national budget. Thus, only further federal expansion would be limited and the amendment's effects on society in general would be minimized.

While the turning point affected by such an amendment would not represent an extremely radical departure from national policy, the broad effort involved in creating and ratifying a Federal Limit Amendment would accomplish a powerful rejuvenation of constitutional principles and philosophy within the society. This would represent the psychological aspect of **recurrence to principle** and if these sentiments were properly nurtured and nationally stimulated, they could lead to much wiser and more effective democratic processes. The process of constitutional amendment itself would create a valuable refocus on the need for effective, constitutional control.

This may stimulate and strengthen the proposal of other creative disciplines to create effective government controls such as:

Pay Go policies that require that every new, proposed expenditure must be funded from new taxes or funds from other parts of the budget.

The Presidential Line Veto that would allow the President to eliminate line item spending from bills.

Term Limits for Representatives would also improve government control attitudes by removing incentives for career politicians.

Add **Sunset Provisions** to existing and all new laws to force periodic review and rejustification of need. This would strengthen congressional oversight and recurrence to principle.

Pass a law that requires that any member of congress voting for a budget in which there is a deficit of more than 3% of GDP (Gross Domestic Product) will be ineligible for re-election.

Proposed Amendment to the United States Constitution: "Congress shall make no law that applies to the citizens of the United States that does not apply equally to the Senators and/or

Representatives; and, Congress shall make no law that applies to the Senators and/or Representatives that does not apply equally to the citizens of the United States."

The Mack Penny Plan would balance the Federal Budget in8 years by cutting one penny out of every federal dollar spent for 6 years and cap spending at 18% of Gross Domestic Product beginning in the 7th year. If congress fails to make the necessary cuts, the plan triggers automatic across-the-board cut to meet the yearly caps.

With a redirection initiated and emphasis being placed on better principles, national leaders would be chosen and would rise to be caretakers of these principles. Such leaders would then guide the people in developing a society that is controlled by a national government that is truly effective, responsive and yet supportive of freedom in the nation. The current low opinion of the members of Congress would certainly improve with these new results and influences.

It may be that current trends to bigger government with more benefits leading to greater and greater national debt will continue given the inability of Congress to make the tough decisions. This will eventually cause Atlas America to shrug and insolvency will occur. It that aftermath, major recurrence to effective principles will have to be done. This is what it may take to finally, seriously consider some of these suggested initiatives.

PART VI

RESULTS AND EFFECTS

Any examination of possible results and effects that might come from the enactment of an amendment such as the proposed Federal Limit Amendment would have to be considered highly academic and theoretical. Never the less, considerable value might result from considering what might happen and what effects could be created. Direct and implicit disciplines would be created by such a limit amendment. A dissertation concerning these disciplines and their effects would probably be useful in gaining insight into these problems of control of government.

The direct disciplines are those that are explicit in the wording of the amendment. They define the creation and control of the federal expenditure limit and the disposition of any excess funds that might be accumulated. These are very direct disciplines and would probably be effective during the initial years after amendment enactment when the sense and intent of the amendment remains clear in the minds of the people.

Almost certainly, however, elements of the Federal Government would ultimately devise schemes for bypassing or nullifying these disciplines just as they have bypassed the checks and balance systems inherent in our original Constitution. Most likely some of the first efforts would be to develop elements of federal spending that are not reported within the controlled budget. When such deviations occur, and certainly they would, the task of **"recurrence to constitutional principle"** would fall again to the citizens and their Representatives. Such guards must be a continuing concern if principles that provide freedom from burdensome government are to prevail.

The passage of a Federal Limit Amendment would also create some new implicit disciplines. Those may well be more important than the direct disciplines in that they would force a change in attitudes within government. With a limit on funds available for federal spending, the administrators would have to take a new look at their methods of obtaining funds. Infinitely expandable tax revenues from economic growth or borrowed funds would no longer be available for their disposition.

Assuming the existence of a limit on federal expenditures, proposals for new governmental functions would have to be carefully examined and justified. Their worth would have to be clearly proven. Such worth would have to be carefully weighed within the priorities of all expenditures. To get funds for these new activities, less worthy governmental functions would have to be reduced or made more efficient and effective. The only source of additional funds would be from other parts of the federal budget. A system of competition among agencies and departments would be created. Federal "pork barrel" or "earmark" projects for certain states would be difficult to develop and harder still to maintain through periods of reevaluation.

Functions that are not clearly justifiable would be put under fire and be made truly valuable or eliminated. Review, justification and periodic re-justification would become functional necessities. A primary question to be asked concerning any new proposals or in reviewing existent functions would be; "Is this function really needed and would this function be better performed at a state or local level?"

Duplication of functions in different agencies would have to be to be reviewed and justified and then eliminated or adjusted.

Functions that are truly federal in nature and truly needed would easily make their cases of justification. If the limit were retained at a given level over a period of years, the addition of new needed federal services would force a return of many of the current functions to the states or be eliminated as they should be. Thus, a proper decentralization of control would be accomplished.

The states would play an important role in influencing decisions on federal functions. Significant financial leverages would be available to the states to obtain and retain control of proper state and local functions. Financing could he made available for valid state and local services either by way of return of limit surpluses or by limit adjustment. Even if these leverages were not exercised, their existence would create vital psychological disciplines on the federal system.

On the other hand, the Federal Government would not be rigidly excluded from operating in areas that could be state or local functions. The liberal interpretation of the "General Welfare" clause would still be in effect. This would enable the Federal Government to guide and influence state and local activities in ways that would truly promote the General Welfare of the Nation.

When problems develop in a number of the states in such a way that they apparently represent or threaten to become a national problem, the Federal Government could exercise its "general welfare" powers. It would be especially prone to use such powers if the states appear to be generally insensitive to the problems. Such problems would be debated in a national forum that would attract wide attention. The states would sense that the Federal Government is considering moving into these areas and this knowledge would energize local and state concern regarding the issues. Then, depending on reactions on both levels, actions would develop that would be influenced by competitive concern. The interaction of federal and state biases would force clear distinctions of proper levels of authority for problem solutions. Not only would effective checks exist, balances and action stimulators would be in operation.

PART VII

PROBLEM EXAMPLES AND POSSIBLE EFFECTS

To gain more insight into the possible effects that a disciplinary Constitutional technique such a Federal Limit Amendment might have, some example problems and related functions of the Federal Government will be considered. It is impossible to predict exactly what might occur due to the interactions set up by the implicit disciplines of a limit amendment. Such uncertainty will probably be true of any effective technique of governmental control. For history has clearly shown that the complexities of large governments quickly invalidate any set of control specifics.

The following subjects will be considered; National Economics (National Debt, "New Economics") Problems of the Cities (Welfare and Urban Redevelopment), Civil Rights, War and a Federal Limit.

NATIONAL ECONOMICS

Fiscal responsibility and the economic health of the nation must be a prime concern of governmental leaders as well as citizens. If fiscal irresponsibility adversely affects national economic wellbeing, then not only is the society in danger of ultimate bad effects but, more immediately, financial resources for dealing with current services and problems can be seriously threatened.

It is in the area of national economics that the expansive, accumulative nature of the Federal Government has been most evident in recent years. Budget deficits are almost habitual and, in more recent years, deficits of hundreds of Billions of dollars are not enough. Often, budgets were not even defined. Trillion dollar deficit authorizations were repeatedly made.

The Federal Debt as of January 2007 was over $8.5 Trillion.

The Federal Debt limit was increased to $9 Trillion in 2008.

The bailouts and stimulus programs of 2008 and 2009 are purely deficit spending. The Federal Debt in April 2009 was $12 Trillion. The limit has again been expanded to$17+ Trillion to accommodate additional expenditures.

The estimated population of the United States is 300,600,000.

Each citizen's share of this debt is over $52,000.

Since the fiscal year began on 1 October 2005, debt has grown $2.03 Billion per day.

Unsuccessful attempts have been made to limit the Federal Public Debt by requiring that the federal budget be balanced.

In 1936, Representative Harold Knutson (MN) proposed the first constitutional amendment to balance the budget (H.J. Res. 579, 74th Cong.). It would have established a per capita limitation on the federal public debt.

1980

Republican Party: "If necessary, the Republican Party will seek to adopt a Constitutional amendment to limit federal spending and balance the budget, except in time of national emergency as determined by a two-thirds vote of Congress."

Democratic Party: "We oppose a Constitutional amendment requiring a balanced budget."

- **1982**

On 4 August, the Senate adopted (69-31) a balanced budget constitutional amendment (S.J. Res. 58 of the 97th Congress). The House did not take up this measure.

- **1985**

Congress passed the Gramm-Rudman-Hollings Act (PL 99-177, Balanced Budget and Emergency Deficit Control Act), which required automatic cuts in discretionary spending.

- **1986**

On 25 March, by one vote the Senate failed (66-34) to adopt a balanced budget constitutional amendment (S.J. Res. 225 of the 99th Congress).

- In September, the House amends Gramm-Rudman-Hollings (P.L. 100-119) and adopts higher deficit levels.

- **1990**

On 17 July, the House failed to achieve a two-thirds majority on H.J. Res. 268, a balanced budget constitutional amendment.

- **1992**

On 9 June, the House failed to achieve a two-thirds majority on a balanced budget constitutional amendment.

- **1994**

On 1 March, the Senate failed (63-37) to pass a balanced budget constitutional amendment (S.J. Res. 41 of the 103rd Congress).

On 17 March, the House failed to achieve a two-thirds majority on a balanced budget constitutional amendment (H.J. Res. 103).

- **1996**

On 26 January, the House passed a balanced budget amendment (300-132).

On 6 June, the Senate failed to pass a balanced budget constitutional amendment (64-35).

- **1997**

On 4 March, the Senate failed (66-34) to achieve a two-thirds majority on a balanced budget constitutional amendment.

On 16 March 2006, Congress raised the debt limit to $9 Trillion. The total debt of the US Federal Government was $8,273,989,918,621.73. That's $27,690.88 for each adult and child in this country (estimated population: 298,798,379).

The debt limit has again been expanded to $17+ Trillions to accommodate the enormous deficits created by the Bush and Obama administrations to counteract the 2008 – 2009 recession.

Regardless of major party affiliation, the national leadership attempts to project an image of concern over federal costs. Each makes token gestures and efforts toward federal fiscal responsibility. But the net effects are clearly evidenced in actual budgetary growth patterns. No plans are even proposed that will actually eliminate the Deficits or reduce the National Debt. Minimal proposals are made that only slow the rate of growth of the Federal Government. Actual cuts are left for future politicians to make.

The 2013 Debt is $17+ Trillion.

By 2020 the debt will likely be over $20 Trillion.

Clearly, legislated Federal spending limits are ineffective. **A specific Constitutional Limit is needed to create a discipline that actually accomplishes real limit control.**

"NEW" ECONOMIC THEORIES

The Keynesian economic theories that gained general academic acceptance and have been implemented since President Kennedy tell us that the Federal Government should "fine tune" the nation's economy along a path of sound growth in line with productivity. Using such theories, we are told will avoid serious recessions and control dangerous inflationary trends. These theories, popularly known at the time as "The New Economics", recommend that the government use the leverages inherent in the Federal Reserve System, tax revenue increases and decreases and budget deficits as well as a technique called "jaw boning" to control runaway tendencies in the nation's economy.

As theory, the "New Economics" seems to make sense and it would seem that it could work if used properly. Unfortunately, the Federal Government shows no inclination to properly use such theories.

The necessities of politics and temptations of political power warp and twist and turn the "New Economics" from seemingly sensible economic theory into a monstrous government generator.

The "New Economics" makes a great point of judiciously using budget deficits to stimulate the economy when recessionary trends seem imminent. Also, tax cuts are recommended under such conditions to get the economy moving. The theory is that small deficits added to the national debt are not dangerous as long as the size of the debt retains a proper relationship to the total capital value of the nation. Certainly no danger would evolve if periodic deficits were counterbalanced with periodic debt retirements from budget surpluses. However, such reasonable actions are not in line with the inherent natural tendencies, characteristics and inclinations of government, politicians and bureaucrats.

Instead we see: *Surpluses* - Quickly absorbed by new functions requiring more government employees, facilities, equipment, etc.

Tax increases - Great reluctance to pass needed tax increases during election years. Devious, gradual taxation increases are accomplished by manipulation of a multitude of tax, fee and tariff sources.

Tax Decreases - Tax decreases are only voted in conjunction with budget deficits to ensure no reduction in governmental functions.

National Debt Increases - Habitual and done in greater increments that are totally unjustifiable in an inflationary economy.

One of the first things President Kennedy did when he entered office was to promote and accomplish a tax decrease to counteract recessionary trends. This was in line with the principles of the "new economics". Of course, this decrease in tax revenue was counterbalanced with a budgetary deficit to avoid any reduction in the scope of the Federal Government. In spite of the fact that the government had to go to the money market to fund its deficit, the tax relief stimulators worked well and the resultant multipliers generated tax revenues in subsequent years. These surpluses were quickly used to expand the role of the Federal Government in the society.

A strong inflationary trend coupled with governmental growth was started. Through this inflationary trend, greater and greater deficits under the Johnson Administration "Great Society" programs added further fuels to inflationary fires. These programs were designed with built-in automatic escalators. Most of this was blamed on the Viet Nam War but, in truth, nonmilitary expenditures of the Federal Government have by far become the major portion of the federal budget.

Tax increases were advocated to stem inflation but effective, meaningful reduction in federal expenditures were impossible to obtain. Indications of future economic peril abound and yet government seems incapable of doing the things that are necessary mainly because these things require reductions in the scope of government.

Historically, effective control of the scope of government has been an impossible accomplishment in democratic societies. All history seems to say that democracies are only satisfactory as temporary forms of government and that they are incapable of sound perpetuation. This nation's founders recognized this fact and developed a system of government with checks and balances that would properly control the role of government in the society. But now, these founding dreams and principles seem to be inadequate. The checks have been slipped and the balances are askew. **A recurrence to principle is required.**

With a Federal Budget Limit in effect, different attitudes toward national economics would have to develop. First, dangerous federal expansionary trends would be checked. The limit would force research into existing operations to provide the financial resources for any new needed functions. Interdepartmental competition would force a much needed house cleaning. Duplication and unneeded departments and functions would be eliminated. Functions that would be better done at state or local levels would be removed from the Federal Government. The elimination of unrestricted opportunity for power assumption and expansion would instill a much more reasoned and moral approach to all phases of government. This would be especially important in the area of national economics.

With the disciplinary influence of an expansion limit functioning, congress could make decisions regarding national economic problems from a position that would not be significantly influenced by biases of federal power expansion. Flagrant attitudes of extravagance could not exist because the finances simply would not be there to support them.

There would be much less danger of inflationary trends developing due to irresponsible national fiscal policies. However, should inflationary situations develop that generate surpluses in federal income beyond the limit, the government would not be able to spend these surpluses. This would eliminate a most significant source of fuel feedback for the economic fires. The Federal Government would not be inclined to do deficit spending during inflationary times for it could not expand its own economic, government (power) base.

It might elect to retire the national debt with such surpluses and may well be inclined to do so as an anti-inflationary measure. If inflation were so rampant as to require tax increases, the revenues from such income increases again could be used against the National Debt to stem inflation. A secondary benefit of this is reduction in interest payments on such debts. Tax income could not be used by the government to create new federal functions whose spending would invalidate inflationary dampening as has been the case in the past.

Should recessionary trends set in, the Federal Government could decide to feed federal funds to the states to stimulate economic activity. Such funds would be borrowed by the issuance of federal bonds and notes in the same way that deficit budget expenditures are now financed. Spending such funds through the states would be in line with proper decentralization of functions thereby getting the greatest effectiveness from these funds. Another method that might be used would be to give a federal tax reduction and make up the difference in the federal income by borrowing procedures. The Important consideration in such economic actions should be that they could be taken for sound economic reasons that would be much less biased from the standpoint of expansion or contraction of the federal power base.

At this point in time, the "New Economics" cannot be said to be proven to be sound and viable principles. The practice of these theories has been badly distorted by political influences and tendencies to federal expansion. The necessities of politics and temptations of political power warp and twist and turn the "New Economics" from seemingly sensible economic theory into a monstrous government generator.

The explicit and implicit disciplines of a "Federal Limit Amendment" would certainly create a better economic and political environment for further testing of the concepts of the "New Economics"

URBAN PROBLEMS

While functioning under a Federal Limit Amendment, how would the government respond to the problems of the cities? Certainly there are problems that require action and solutions. They are widely discussed. They are real and clearly apparent. Air and water pollution, congestion, core city decay, obsolescence or transportation and education systems not to mention a host of serious, special problems that are unique to given areas or localities. The funds required to solve these problems run into the hundreds of Billions of dollars and will represent a continual drain on the economy for the foreseeable future.

The Federal Government is deeply involved and is spending Billions annually to attack these problems. The Department Of Health Education and Welfare which was created by Congressional enactment in 1953 has grown to become a major department with a budget running into the tens of Billions of dollars.

The problems of the cities are immense in scale and infinitely varied in complexity and nature. The solutions required must be similarly varied and accordingly scaled and tailored to fit local situations. If they are to be effective solutions that truly satisfy the problems and people involved, they will probably not; come out of any mold fashioned in Washington. These problems are different in all cities just as all cities are different. The natures of cities and their problems are as unique as their individual geographies, their terms of existence, and the ethnic and cultural backgrounds of their people.

Detroit has recently declared bankruptcy. It has terrible economic and cultural problems. Recently Senator Rand Paul made news by proposing a wide-ranging plan to revitalize the nation's cities through the creation of "economic freedom zones." His plan would cut federal taxes in communities that have an unemployment rate of 12% or more.

Federal personal and corporate taxes would be lowered to 5%, and the federal payroll tax would be cut to 2% each for employees and employers.

"Inside these zones, we'll suspend the capital gains tax and allow small businesses to deduct most of what they invest," he said.

The plan would save Detroit $1.3 billion over the next 10 years, Paul said.

This is an example of the type of new, innovative thinking that is required to deal with the complex problems in cities. Detroit is not the only city with serious fiscal problems. There are many others. The Federal Government is clearly incapable of providing the solutions to these problems.

Often the solutions to city problems require the exercise of rights of eminent domain where government forcefully takes ownership of a private property to make a more public beneficial use of it. People must be uprooted and moved. Such work is always delicate and requires a high degree of precise skill and concern to minimize the painful, costly human effects and to endure that just actions are taken. This is no work for the "Federal Bulldozer". The decisions as to need, initiation, method, extent and timing clearly belong at the local and state levels. The vast costs associated with solutions for the problems of the cities dictate that efficiency in accomplishment is imperative. Extensive decision hierarchies and paper mills cannot be tolerated. The enormous sums of money required should not be routed through Washington for bureaucratic depletion, delay and misdirection.

With a Federal Limit Amendment in effect, state and local governments would receive federal revenues above the limit figure in addition to normal Federal funds. Such excess funds would be dispensed at the state level on a per capita basis which is not only equitable but suitable to the populous nature of the problems. Such dispensations, free of Washington's discounts and interferences, could be applied in a decentralized manner according to real area and local needs.

Given continued growth in the GDP (Gross National Product) and a Fixed Federal Limit, increasing revenue excesses should prove adequate to meet the problems of population growth and to accomplish the adjustments and renovations needed to save and maintain our cities.

CIVIL RIGHTS

Creation of racial fraternity through the use of governmentally administered economics and legal force is indeed a dangerous experiment. The relatively limited experience we have had with the Federal Government attempting to legislate interracial harmony has clearly demonstrated the truth in Fredrick Bastiat's warning;

"If you attempt to make the law fraternal, equalizing, you will then be lost in an uncharted territory, in vagueness and uncertainty, in a Forced utopia. This is true because fraternity and philanthropy, unlike justice, do not have precise limits. Once started, where will you stop and where will the law stop itself?"

Not only are we beginning to see the "uncharted Federal utopias" but dangerous evidences of interracial and interclass warfare develop.

Still, there is undeniable truth in the charges of discrimination and bigotry leveled during the years of strife over civil rights. The minority races have been unjustly dealt with and such treatment must be condemned. Clearly there is a role for government in dealing with intolerance and injustice to minorities. Experience would indicate, however, that the role should be one of moral and ethical leadership rather than force in creation of fraternity among citizens. Plenty of laws and rulings have already been made to protect civil rights.

Bigotry and intolerance are ingrained and emotional characteristics that suppressive legal force is more likely to inflame rather than subdue. If these evil human faults are to be ultimately eliminated, it must be done through leadership in example and by ethical persuasion. Most importantly, the persecuted minorities must prove by their actions and lives that the biases are unjustified and unconscionable. Time and the good influences of leadership and example are the only possible ultimate remedies for the inequities. While it is difficult for the persecuted minorities to accept this, it is the only way. The alternatives of dependency programs, use of force and legal bribery have led and will continue to lead to damaging actions that will ultimately hurt the afflicted minorities the most. Such solutions may prove to be infinitely worse than the problems.

By making funds more available and more effective at local levels, perhaps the problems of housing for ghetto dwellers will be better handled. Instead of creating vast jungles of Federal housing projects, a closer relationship to the people can be developed. Through more intimate contacts and flexibilities that can adapt to local human needs, solutions that work may be attainable.

A Federal Limit Amendment would probably affect a gradual shift of present federal welfare and educational functions back to the states. Since these are basically and properly state and local functions, the states would likely move to control the federal limit so as to force these functions back to the states. Thus the basic elements of force would be removed from the Federal Government in these matters. However, this would not restrict the role of federal leadership in civil rights. A national forum would still exist to advocate resolution of inequalities.

Where severe conditions of injustice exist so as to arouse the national conscience, special functions of economic and legal force could be created and utilized. Once such functions have served their purpose, they would be eliminated to provide the funds to satisfy other national needs and affected state or states then would proceed in a more enlightened manner.

WAR AND A FEDERAL LIMIT AMENDMENT

The Military Industrial Complex

Where in the world is our Military? In 144 nations according to an article in the American Legion Magazine, Some of the largest are:

Republic of S. Korea 27,000
Japan 50,000
Iraq (15,00 in Embassy 2012)
Kuwait 16,000
Hawaii 35,000

Afghanistan	66,000
United Kingdom	10,000
Germany	58,000
Italy	10,000
Alaska	19,000
Continental US	876,000
At sea/in port	115,000

Consider the industry, logistics, facilities and equipment costs to support the Military Complex. The proposed 2013 Federal Military Budget is $650 Billion.

President Eisenhower, at the end of his term, warned us of the dangers inherent in the power and influence or what he called a "*military industrial complex*" in our society. Collusion between government and war industry is not new but it is always dangerous and must be carefully controlled in a free society. A proper limit to defense and national security expenditures is essential.

In Section 8 of the US Constitution which defines the fiscal powers of the Federal Government, its power to fund the Military is described:

To raise and support armies, but no appropriation of money to that use shall be for a longer term than two years.

In fact no budget of any kind has been passed by the Senate in over three years.

With a federal budget limit In effect, this nation would be a great deal more careful and justified in entering into international conflict than it has been. Clear reasons would have to develop and be explicitly enunciated by federal leaders to arouse a definite national purpose and thereby cause the states to expand the federal limit. With a federal limit in effect, great pressures would always exist within the national government to utilize all Defense Department and available federal funds. With this situation existing, only wars of absolute necessity and clearest justification would be authorized and fought. Wars would have to be justified with a clear enemy or threat and defined with clear goals and exit strategies.

The limit amendment would require a simple majority of state legislatures to support necessary limit expansions. This support would have to be renewed annually to provide continuing funds. Thus, two new checks are created on national war making potential. Specific control of the defense system, the responsibility for national security and the initiative of defining the necessity of war would still reside with the national government.

Where a war is justified, obtaining initial approval by the states would not be difficult and, for as long as the war should be fought, support would be forthcoming. When such a war is finished though, an especially important aspect of the limit amendment would take effect. With the need for war removed, the limit could revert to prewar status at which time the Congress could vote the released funds for deficit reduction, a tax reduction or release the funds for dispersion to the states. Too often in the past, war's end has meant that funds needed for defense during war are used to expand the role of the Federal Government in the society.

The Second World War was a prime example of this process. From 1940 to 1950 the federal budget more than tripled in size. The premise that a tax cut can also stimulate a postwar economy is not given strong consideration at such times. The idea that defense spending must be re-channeled into an expansion of peaceful governmental functions always has prevailed. A federal limit would eliminate the "greater government" biases at those critical times thereby fostering a much healthier post war adjustment environment.

It is doubtful that the Vietnam, Iraq and Afghanistan wars would have been started or long supported with this type of amendment in effect. Surely the Iraq war would never have been authorized or supported especially as the sectarian violence escalated after Sadam's fall. Support for the war in Afghanistan would be doubtful given the historic failures by Britain and Russia to succeed there. Using the military for Nation Building would be very difficult to support and sustain.

The massive government expenditures and controls authorized by the "War On Terror" would never have gone to the extremes allowed with a limit amendment in effect. The term "War On Terror" is a good example of the technique of over exaggeration of a threat to justify enormous government expansion. A "War On Terror" will likely never see a definable end. Terror is a reaction and terrorism is a tactic not a nation state to be attacked. One cannot wage war on a reaction or tactic to any satisfactory conclusion. Terrorism has been practiced throughout history and will be with us in the future in one form or another. Terrorists consist of small groups or cells scattered around the world. As such they should be fought when they pose a real threat identified with intelligence investigations and attacked with surgical Special Forces strikes when warranted given accurate intelligence.

THE ROLE OF POLITICAL PARTIES

Theodore Roosevelt had this to say about political parties in his day:

"The old parties are husks, with no real soul within either, divided on artificial lines, boss-ridden and privilege-controlled, each a jumble of incongruous elements, and neither daring to speak out wisely and fearlessly on what should be said on the vital issues of the day."

This could be descriptive of the Republican and Democratic parties today. Both of these parties are focused on gaining control of the Federal Government and the enormous budget and power that comes with it. Both parties have increased the size of the Federal Government when in control and show no sign of changing these patterns. $ Trillion budget deficits have been routinely accepted. The pursuit of government power has corrupted both parties. The two parties differ little in this respect except that the Democrats tend to do more domestic spending while the Republicans favor policies that support business and military expenditures. Both parties accept and are influenced by extensive funding from lobbyists and corporate and military industry interests.

Earmark projects, otherwise known as "pork" projects, have proliferated in recent years. There were more earmarks in 2005 than from 1991 to 1999 combined. Although the number of earmarks went down in 2006, their cost increased $6 Billion in one year -- from $23 Billion in 2005 to $29 Billion in 2006. Many earmarks are not included in the bills, but rather in non-binding conference or committee reports.

In 2006, Republicans showed complete disregard of fiscal responsibility when earmarks exceeded 25,000.

Republicans promoted an image of fiscal conservatism favoring lower taxes and reduction of government functions. This image was destroyed in the 2006 election by their abandonment of fiscal responsibility. When the Republicans came to control the Presidency and the legislative branches with majorities, access to all that money and power turned them into bigger spenders than the Democrats. The Iraq and Afghanistan wars were unfunded. President Bush added to the problem by never vetoing any Republican spending bill thereby allowing unprecedented deficits to be created. They further damaged their image with the deficit funded Medicare Drug program and the first of the TARP bank bailouts and enormous federal debt increases.

When the Republicans succumbed to these attractions, they lost their reputation as the party of constitutional small government and low taxes and thereby they lost the Conservative faithful. Republicans did not change government, government changed the party. The question for the Republicans now is, can they reestablish their previous reputation in a believable way?

THE LIBERTARIAN PARTY

The most significant 3rd party in the nation is the Libertarian Party. They run candidates for local, state and Federal offices. But their success has been very limited to a few state and federal victories. They propose a very limited role for governments that protects free exchange and prevents illegal actions. They did receive 13 million votes in the 2006 elections. Ron Paul, the current strong proponent of Libertarian principles has a dedicated and significant following. However Libertarian Party appeal is not broad enough to have major national or state impacts.

Recognizing problems with political parties, Fredrick Bastiat said this: *"I have taken the decision that, whatever happens, I will not be a Party man."*

Some suggest that, in order to get the Federal Senators and Representatives to clearly recognize that the people are clearly alarmed by the expansion of the Federal Government and the enormous debts being created, all incumbents should be voted out of office with no regard to party affiliation. This would definitely deliver the message of desired change. It may be an alternative to conservative third party support which often simply dilutes Republican support and causes Democrats to be elected.

What must be accomplished in our society today is a general, public re-evaluation and re-assessment of the original system of checks and balances, with special consideration being given to why they failed and how they or others which are more effective can be re-established and effectively maintained. A necessary preliminary to such actions would be the accomplishment of a re-awakening of the people to the vital importance of such disciplines in any system of government and to the dangers inherent in any system where they do not exist.

In Article 15 of the Virginia Declaration of Rights, which was drafted by George Mason and adopted in 1776, appears this statement:

"No free government or the blessings of liberty can be preserved to any people but by firm adherence to justice, moderation, temperance, frugality, and

*virtue and by **frequent recurrence to fundamental principles.*** **The time for "recurrence" is long overdue.**

What is clear is that if the Republican Party continues in its disregard to constitutional principles and support of fiscally irresponsible policies it will become an irrelevant party and will be replaced with a new one based on Independent Constitutional principles. Unfortunately this may only develop after national insolvency occurs.

All of the budget plans currently proposed by the Democrats or Republicans only address reducing the budget deficit (the amount over a balanced budget). These plans only slow the amount of budget growth. They propose reducing the deficit over a 10 year period. No meaningful cuts are made now.

These plans require that future legislators must do the actual cutting. A very dubious assumption.

None of the current plans actually reduce the $17+ Trillion current national debt. In fact, even if the proposed cuts are actually done over the 10 year period, $7 – 8 Trillion more will be added to the debt increasing it to over $20 Trillion because budgets will not be balanced during this period with current proposed plans. The current $17+

Trillion national debt is larger than all the European economies combined. How long can this go on? How will our children deal with these generational debt burdens?

If the Federal Debt is ever to be reduced, the first requirement is to balance the Federal Budget by eliminating the annual deficits. What is the deficit? It is the amount by which the Federal Government outlays exceeds its total outlays for a fiscal year.

Recent   US   Federal Deficits

Obama Deficits

Bush Deficits

FY 2012: $1,089 Billion

FY 2009: $1,413 Billion

FY 2011: 2011

Billion

FY 2008: $459

Billion

FY 2010: 1,293

Billion

FY 2007: $161

Billion

The National Debt will continue to grow as long as deficits continue to add to it. So the key question is, how can the Federal Budget be balanced? It will require elimination or reduction of many of the current operations of the Federal Government. In many cases, the operations may be returned to the States to assume their correct role in these operations. **A recurrence to Constitutional Principles will be required.**

Fiscal insolvency will occur when the interest on the national debt seriously erodes the funds available to meet national budgetary requirements. The low current interest rates disguise the debt interest problem that rising interest rates will bring.

Current Interest rates on U.S. bonds are currently low, but that doesn't mean the country's future interest payments on the national debt will be. The government will pay out more than $5 trillion in interest payments over the next decade, according to the latest projections from the Congressional Budget Office.

Over the decade, more than 14% of *all revenue* the government is projected to collect will be paid out in interest payments. That's a lot of money that cannot be used on the country's other priorities.

Indeed, between 2013 and 2022, estimated interest costs will be:

Higher than Medicaid spending;

Equal to half of Social Security spending;

Close to what is spent on all of Defense.

The estimated interest costs assume a fairly steady and moderate increase in rates over the decade.

The CBO assumes that the yield on the 10-year Treasury will rise from an estimated current 2.3% 5% by the end of the decade; and the yield on the 3-month T-bill will increase from 0.1% to 3.8% during the same time.

With the Federal Reserve continuing "Quantitative Easing", printing money, to fund continuing debt this fiat money is bound to eventually cause inflation. The Fed will then increase interest rates to combat inflation. Interest payments are immediate demands on the Federal Budget thereby increasing deficits adding to the National Debt or drastically cutting into other spending.

These interest payment potentials represent the greatest danger leading to national insolvency.

The best potential for surviving these debt crises is by supporting powerful growth of the national economy. This must be stimulated by tax incentive and limiting regulation policies that will generate such expansion.

LIFE CHANGING POTENTIALS

Energy production, computing, nano technology and new material development, have the potentials to change the world as we know it at an exponential, unpredictable rate.

ENERGY ECONOMIC POTENTIALS

The greatest growth potential exists in positive expansion of energy resources. The US has the potential to become energy independent and energy rich if national policies and incentives focus on such resources. Oil, natural gas, coal, nuclear must all be supported and promoted. Solar and wind power generation can also be supported as they develop and becomes economically competitive.

Natural gas is an efficient energy source and the cleanest-burning fossil fuel. Natural gas extracted from dense shale rock formations has become the fastest-growing source of gas in the United States. Energy companies have combined two established technologies—hydraulic fracturing and horizontal drilling to successfully unlock energy recources. The U.S. Energy Information Administration (EIA) estimates the United States possesses more than 2,500 Trillion cubic feet of technically recoverable natural gas resources, of which 33 percent is held in shale rock formations. Natural gas from shale has grown to 25 percent of U.S. gas production in just a decade and will be 50 percent by 2035, according to the EIA. Developing this resource can help enhance energy security and strengthen economies. As the distribution infrastructure for delivery and wide scale use of this energy resource in transportation is accomplished, the economy will benefit enormously.

An energy rich and independent US will not only contribute to the economic growth necessary to correct its fiscal debt crises, it will also allow reduced terrorist dangers. The US will no longer be threatened by the instability and hostility of mid-east petroleum suppliers.

THE EFFECTS OF THE POWER OF THE POWER OF COMPUTING

Another force that will powerfully strengthen and stimulate the economy is the continuing acceleration of the speed and power of computers.

Gordon Moore, a CEO of the Intel Corporation manufacturer of computer and memory chips defined the nature of the evolution of computer power.

Moore's law *is the observation that over the history of computing hardware, the number of transistors on integrated circuits doubles approximately every two years.*

This means that computers decrease in size and double in speed and memory capacity every 2 years. What is amazing is that this improvement in computer power is likely to continue for the foreseeable future.

The influence of this multiplying computer power has the potential to accelerate the productivity and expansion of the US economy as well as world interconnectivity. It is impossible to predict what or how this will influence this nation and the world. But surely it will have a powerful effect on society and economic potentials. As computing power proliferates and is integrated into products more and more control and intelligence increases their value. Robotics and 3D printing of products and parts will become more capable increasing accuracy, speed and productivity thereby vastly improving manufacturing efficiencies. As computing power is further integrated into transportation, vehicles and roads, safety and efficiencies will be greatly improved.

Nano-technology is the manipulation of matter on an atomic and molecular scale. Generally, nanotechnology works with materials, devices, and other structures with at least one dimension sized from 1 to 100 nanometers. Quantum mechanical effects are important at this quantum-realm scale. With a variety of potential applications, nanotechnology is a key technology for the future.

Graphene is the world's new wonder material. It's the thinnest electronic material ever invented, consisting of a layer of carbon atoms just a single atom thick -- the atoms are arranged in a hexagonal pattern. It weighs almost nothing, coming in at only 0.77 grams for a square meter.

Graphene is 100 times stronger than steel of the same thickness. It conducts both heat and electricity better than copper, and has outstanding optical and mechanical properties. Initially this will mean that graphene is used to help improve the performance and efficiency of current materials and substances. In the future it will also be developed with other two-dimensional (2D) crystals to create some even more amazing compounds.

As nano-technology and micro computing is incorporated with new materials, many fields will evolve in life changing ways that are incomprehensible today.

PART VIII

THE GREATEST NEED

The suggested Federal Limit Amendment is an example of a corrective measure that could be taken. It is presented to illustrate the principles discussed. It could be done to perform the function of **"Recurrence to Fundamental Principles"** which is essential to the maintenance of a free society. If something like it cannot be reasonably accomplished in today's political climate, it may be more of a last resort kind of action that would be more feasible after occurrence of national fiscal insolvency.

Examinations and thought which will find ways to effectively perform '"recurrence to principle" represents the greatest lack in the present day American political society. Even disciplines such as Pay-Go policies which require that every new expenditure must be funded from other parts of the budget or the Presidential Line Veto which would allow the President to eliminate line item spending form bills that he signs are not used. Term limits for representatives would also improve government control attitudes by removing incentives for career politicians. Also adding "sunset provisions" to laws to force periodic review and rejustification of need would strengthen congressional oversight and recurrence to principle but are seldom included in legislation.

Most prevailing political and governmental thought is polarized with either the "progressive (liberal) greater government" or "conservative limited government" philosophies. The major choices are between two extremes. We must stop the wild oscillations between these extremes. Both extremes have serious faults that are clearly recognizable. Creative minds that can fill the vacuum in between these extremes represent this nation's greatest need.

Liberals (now known as Progressives) have been extremely effective in promoting positive images for their causes in the public's mind. For example, all government spending is now call investment. This positive image has been mainly accomplished because their causes have been responsive to problems. They are really no more humane people than conservatives. Liberals are simply liberal in their willingness to use governmental funds and force to solve problems. For this they are applauded by those who receive the help; the bureaucrats, and politicians who administer the services, a supportive media and a gullible taker citizenry. They irresponsibly advocate "greater government" as the panacea for all social ills with no regard for potential dangers inherent in the fiscal dangers they turn loose. Solve the problems, they cry. The end would justify the means. Disregard that the funding needed for such programs are irresponsibly provided.

Problems must be solved but badly conceived and deficit funded and poorly administered solutions can have broader and more terrible effects than the problems themselves. Do liberals really deserve the positive image they enjoy? Definitely not, for they have let their compassions run away with, their common sense.

They have forgotten George Washington's admonition that government can also be a "fearful master".

Libertarian principles, except for civil liberties, have been left to the conservatives for advocacy and defense. Conservative negativism has too often served to hide the lights of liberty under clouds of unconstructive governmental criticism, problematic disregard, paranoid anti-communism and anti-terrorism. If Constitutional principles are to be effective in America, they must be placed in a new context of governmental philosophy that stresses the positive aspects of compassion and sensitivity to problems. This philosophy must advocate principles that foster an effective, responsive and freedom supporting government through processes of automatic adjustment and functional leveling that need not rely on a consistent critical citizenry for their operation.

This is not only a challenge for those of a conservative or libertarian mind. It is a challenge for all who believe in Constitutional government and the American dream of freedom for the individual. It is probably the most important question facing America today and it is especially significant for the younger generation.

It may well be that the young people sense that the root principles of our society no longer have validity and, in the questioning manner of youth, they are rebelling against the old concepts of government. They correctly believe that the enormous debts that they will have to deal with in their generation will drastically limit their potential for success. Few believe that Social Security will be available for them. Their searching is disorganized and they have no clear goals in mind. It is here submitted that a goal worthy of all possible efforts would be the invention and creation of Constitutional principles that provide effective, responsive government functioning in a society that retains maximum freedom for the individual.

American principles of freedom and free markets have created the greatest, most successful nation in the history of the world. With effective recurrence to constitutional government that is effective and responsive, an even better, shining example of an ideal society can be provided to the world. Rather than promoting such a society's principles through force and ineffective nation building campaigns, let other societies be persuaded by an excellent, successful national example.

We are at a medieval stage in terms of intelligent use and control of government in society. Our ability to design and implement new, functional systems of governmental control will determine whether we now move into a dark age of smothering, fiscal bankruptcy, irresponsible socialistic over government, dependency and an eventual end to the "American dream".

Can we evaluate the past and from this evaluation reform the principles of freedom and government thereby giving a new vitality and concern to American politics? Creative minds that can provide answers to fill the vacuum between right and left extremism constitute this nation's greatest present need. Hopefully, such a need cannot go unfulfilled.

Is mankind always to be manipulated and ultimately overwhelmed by governmental processes? This question is especially pertinent for Americans today. Certainly the evidence of history relating to the pattern of social governmental evolution and destruction must eventually move mankind to develop effective control systems. For America, the question is valid and, as yet, unanswered. Will we be capable of breaking the cycle or will we remain apathetic and insensitive and follow it to its deadening socialistic/dependent end or worse?

Man, as a creative, intelligent being, certainly has the capacity to devise functional, effective methods of government. This is clearly proven in any examination of the myriad governmental forms and innovations created through history. The American Constitution is an example of a giant step taken toward concepts of balanced, ideal, free government. So it would seem very realistic that an effort could be made again based on our recent experiences and all the examples of history. **A "recurrence to principles" is not only possible, it is essential for survival**.

Our current path of fiscal irresponsibility which is leading to a National Debt that is greater than our Annual Gross Domestic Product and future spending projections that could actually lead to national Insolvency. As $ inflation and interest rates rise, the need to pay these rates required to sustain the massive national debt will drastically impact the nation's ability to meet its required expenditures. **Continuing down this path, Atlas America will have to shrug off the weight of the world. It will have no choice.**

Our ancestors passed on the principles of liberty relatively intact to us. The greatest damages to these principles have been done with in the past forty years. It is probably not yet too late for a **"recurrence to fundamental principles"**, a **Return To Constitutional Federal Government.** It may be too late before very long.

What will we pass on to our grandchildren; massive, uncontrollable government and unsustainable national debts? Will this still be a nation founded on Constitutional principles of effective government in a free society? Will Abraham Lincoln's description of America having "Government of the people, by the people and for the people" still apply? With awareness, concern and action it can be so.

Who is B, J. Galt?

B. J. Galt is the pseudonym of a retired Computer System Engineer. He has published three books defining how end users can be designers of major applications. He originated the design of a computer software system which was responsible for >$3 Billion in system sales for a major corporation.

This book describes the author's reflections, concerns and recommendations based on over 40 years of observance of large, corporate bureaucracy and political history. As a past Conservative and Republican, he now describes himself as a Constitutional Independent. The book represents his evolved, current, political perspectives. It suggests solutions and initiatives to accomplish a **"recurrence to constitutional principles"** thereby returning Constitutional powers to the states and providing for a Federal Government that is fiscally sound, effective in its operations and responsive to the nation's needs while restoring liberty to the individual, dignity to the legislature and purpose to the ballot box.

The Presentation document,
"Constitutional Independent On Point",
summarizes the key points made in the
book:

Constitutional Independent

A State Ratified Federal Limit
Amendment, Need A 3rd Party?
Constitutional Federal Government

Printed copies of the presentation and the
book are available at:
https://www.createspace.com

Also on Kindle & at Amazon Books

ISBN-13 978-1499329964

ISBN-10 1499329962

Email request a Free summary Video or
PDF
B. J. Galt Email: bjongalt@gmail.com

www.ingramcontent.com/pod-product-compliance
Lightning Source LLC
Chambersburg PA
CBHW070840310526
45793CB00010B/112